ABOUT THE AUTHORS

Robert Hiebeler is the Managing Director of KnowledgeSpace, Arthur Andersen's innovative approach to leveraging knowledge for its professionals and its clients. Over the past five years, he has pioneered the development and deployment throughout Arthur Andersen of the Global Best Practices knowledge base, an effort that has captured best-practice information from around the world in key business processes. In addition to leading several worldwide productivity and quality initiatives within Arthur Andersen, he has consulted with hundreds of companies worldwide about the search for, and implementation of, best practices to improve business performance. He lives in Chicago, Illinois.

Thomas B. Kelly is the Managing Partner of Arthur Andersen Knowledge Enterprises, a business focused on electronic commerce and Internet-related knowledge opportunities. He is also Managing Director of Arthur Andersen operations west of the Rocky Mountains and a member of the firm's global management team. His career with Arthur Andersen spans thirty years and three continents, and includes assignments with clients in government, finance, manufacturing, and retailing. He has worked with organizations in the United States, Europe, South America, and Australia on strategic consulting and research projects as well as the design and implementation of business systems. He lives in San Francisco, California.

Charles Ketteman is the Managing Partner of Arthur Andersen's Business Consulting practice. His responsibilities include overall direction of the practice, research efforts for new products and services, and management of global alliances and partner relationships. He has more than twenty years of experience in consulting with clients in a wide range of industries. Most recently, his clients have been primarily concentrated in the telecommunications industry in the U.S. and Asia. He has helped clients make wide-ranging changes and develop new marketing and market expansion strategies, both domestically and internationally. He lives in Dallas, Texas.

BEST
PRACTICES

BUILDING YOUR BUSINESS
WITH CUSTOMER-FOCUSED SOLUTIONS

ROBERT HIEBELER,
THOMAS B. KELLY, AND
CHARLES KETTEMAN

ARTHUR ANDERSEN

SIMON & SCHUSTER

First published in Great Britain by Simon & Schuster UK Ltd, 1998
This paperback edition first published by Simon & Schuster UK Ltd, 1999
A Viacom company

1 3 5 7 9 10 8 6 4 2

Simon & Schuster UK Ltd
Africa House
64-78 Kingsway
London WC2B 6AH

Simon & Schuster Australia
Sydney

A CIP catalogue record for this book is available from the British Library

ISBN 0-684-86035-X

Printed and bound in Great Britain by Caledonian International Book
Manufacturing, Glasgow

CONTENTS

FOREWORD

More than six years ago Arthur Andersen made a decision to invest in creating a process classification system that would allow us to study companies and organizations worldwide and begin collecting "Best Practices" as we encountered them. It was one of the best business decisions we have made during my tenure as managing partner of our practice throughout the Americas. Simply defined, Best Practices are the best ways to perform a business process. We raised questions when surveying how companies sharpen their focus to establish excellence in customer relationships, and among them are the following:

- What is the best way to respond to customer service issues?
- How can those requests be met most effectively?
- What do best-practice companies do to find and train employees to serve customers best?
- How can a company team with customers to design, improve, market, and distribute its products and services?
- What is the most efficient and productive method of tracking and using information about customers and their purchasing patterns, attitudes, and loyalty?

The classification system we created to house Best Practices was based on the major processes that all businesses share, including:

- Understanding markets and customers;
- Designing products and services;
- Marketing and selling those products and services;
- Producing what customers need and want;
- Delivering products and services;
- Serving customers.

Linking Best Practices to processes allowed us to take the best ideas out of the restrictive contexts that limit how people think about business. Those limitations can cause business managers to assume, for instance, that human resource directors can learn only from other human resource directors, or that large companies—in particular industries, in specific places—must be similarly constrained. Focusing on universal processes is a key enabler in breakthrough thinking.

My hope is that this book will help readers as individuals to strengthen their own habits of searching for Best Practices. This book contains some of the finest examples of Best Practices that Arthur Andersen has gathered through the work of more than 50,000 employees worldwide. Leadership in pulling those examples together has been provided by Robert Hiebeler, Managing Director of KnowledgeSpace; Thomas B. Kelly, Managing Partner of Knowledge Enterprises; and Charles Ketteman, Managing Partner of Business Consulting.

A list of others who have provided thought leadership in various Best Practice processes is provided on the following pages.

James D. Edwards
Managing Partner
Arthur Andersen—Americas

ACKNOWLEDGMENTS

Any acknowledgment in this book must begin with the Arthur Andersen organization. To those forward-thinking leaders who believed in, encouraged, and supported our efforts for the past six years in identifying and collecting Best Practices, we owe a fundamental thank-you. Without their support, this book would not exist.

We thank those individuals who helped make this book a reality: Harry Wallace, who conceived and championed the idea for the book and has been key to the process from start to finish; Kathy Iversen and Joe O'Leary, Business Consulting Partners, who provided thought leadership for customer excellence, who shared their experience with us, and who made invaluable suggestions to the book's content; David Shevenaugh, who served as project manager; Stephanie Mantis and the Global Best Practices Team, who provided much research support; Ed Wertzberger, Paul Rukenbrod, Bob Weinstein, and Jim Trinnaman, who worked with the companies featured in this book; Jody Fergerson, who provided proofreading and editorial assistance; and Kitty

Rainey and Viviane Wilcutts, who served admirably as executive assistants.

We are also grateful to the talented writers and editors at Wordworks, Inc., Christina Braun, Maurice Coyle, Erik Hansen, Martha Lawler, Helen Rees, Katie Schofield, Saul Wisnia, and G. Patton Wright, and especially our mentor, Donna Sammons Carpenter. Through their talented efforts they have shown that the pen can be truly mighty. Our senior editor at Simon & Schuster, Fred Hills, believed in this project and gave us much encouragement along the way. For his support we are particularly grateful.

And we offer a special thanks to those individuals and companies cited in the book for their time, patience, and efforts to bring these best practices to readers worldwide.

INTRODUCTION

In *Best Practices*, we share our views on the secrets behind the success of many of today's leading businesses. After years of studying our clients and watching them perfect their best practices, we and our colleagues at Arthur Andersen believe that best practices do not belong to any single company or industry but have universal application to companies large and small across all industries. The search for best practices is all about looking outside yourself. To do this, however, you need to have a common business framework, which we call a process view, to make this happen.

Here are some of the insights we have uncovered:

- Nike, Inc.

Over a two-year period, Nike increased its total sales to women from 15 percent to 65 percent. How? It created an advertising campaign that focused on women. Blasting social stereotypes, the provocative campaign called Dialogue presented women as powerful and capable individuals in print ads running as long as 18 pages.

- DHL (Malaysia)

DHL (Malaysia) has grown from a staff of four to become one of the largest air-express couriers in the country, processing over 3 million orders annually. How? DHL established "ExpressLine," an online service that lets customers order immediate pickups. These orders become part of a company-wide integrated information system that enables DHL not only to monitor the status of any delivery but also to collect and organize information about its customers for better service.

- The Ritz-Carlton Company

The Ritz-Carlton is the only hotel chain to receive a Malcolm Baldrige National Quality Award. What did the chain do to merit this prestigious honor? Among its many other accomplishments, the company stipulates that every Ritz-Carlton hotel compile daily reports covering 720 work-related tasks. Hotel managers measure, for instance, how much time housekeepers need to clean a room. A bellboy overhearing a customer's wish for extra towels reports the information to a supervisor, who sees that the order is carried out. Each point-of-contact employee carries a notebook to record customer preferences and complaints, which are entered into the company's database for constant monitoring.

- American Express

A boycott in 1991 to protest what one Boston restaurateur perceived as American Express's arrogance and inflexibility led the company to a complete evaluation of its customer services operations. Three years later the company had added 350,000 new merchant customers, who received lower rates and better service. How did the company accomplish such a turnaround? It began meeting face-to-face with dissatisfied customers on a daily basis and partnering with merchant customers to offer discounts and special rewards to end users making their purchases with an American Express card.

- Varian Associates, Inc.

In 1997, VSLI Research, Inc., a marketing research company, named Palo Alto–based Varian Associates the top company in customer satisfaction among semiconductor manufacturers and suppliers worldwide. How did Varian win so many satisfied customers? In planning and developing some of its most sophisticated spectroscopy products, the company initiated focus groups in North America, Europe, and Australia that comprised *competitors' customers* as well as Varian's own clients. Varian integrates those customer insights into the development of its new products, thereby making the products easier to use and better suited to customer needs.

- Robert Bosch GmbH

The world's leading manufacturer of electronic automobile components such as antilock brakes, fuel injection systems, and airbags, Robert Bosch GmbH sets a high priority on creating faultless products. Its Eisenach facility, for example, in one year reduced the number of faulty products to only 300 per million. How does the company do it? It creates cross-functional teams of employees who "own" all manufacturing and distribution processes, overseeing every detail during the production process and along the supply chain.

In addition, the company puts prospective employees through a rigorous unpaid training program, with no guarantee of a job at the program's end. For three hours a night over fourteen weeks, candidates study the company's history, learn management techniques, take skills tests, undergo interviews with supervisors, and learn how to better serve customers. Any apprentice missing two classes is dismissed from the program.

- Holy Cross Hospital

In the period 1991–94, Chicago's Holy Cross Hospital went from being ranked in the bottom 5 percent of hospitals in the

United States to a ranking in the top 5 percent. How? It created nine "Commando Teams"—made up of employees from throughout the hospital—to identify and correct any problem its customers experience. One team is responsible solely for identifying barriers to prompt customer service, such as unwarranted wait time in any department. Now in the hospital's imaging department, for example, no patient can be kept waiting more than ten minutes.

In *Best Practices,* we detail the innovations of more than 40 companies, focusing on how those companies identify customers, survey them for their perceptions of the services and products they offer, and seek to understand their needs. Moreover, from investigating literally hundreds of organizations worldwide, we have formed a six-stage schema for incorporating the customer-oriented processes that these best-practice companies have developed to improve services, build partnerships, and secure loyal customers.

Most business books today promise managers a silver bullet—a breakthrough theory or application that in one fell swoop can banish all problems. Instead of having to worry about improving operations, simply change horses and do everything differently. But the reality is that change tends to be incremental; quantum leaps are rare.

We do not claim that this book can give you a silver bullet. It does, however, present a new way of approaching business problems and, more important, a new way to solve them. The chapters that follow range widely over the landscape of business processes. Each chapter is rich in best-practice cases and applications. Each includes a series of best practices for a particular process and the characteristics that made those practices best. They have been selected based on our own firsthand experience and the judgment of those companies' peers. Almost to an organization, the best are dependent for their very existence on achieving excellence in that process, and they own a number of the best practices we list in that category.

In addition, at the end of each chapter we present a best-practice agenda summarizing the primary features of that chapter's process. We conclude with a diagnostic, a list of in-depth questions that probe your company's operations in terms of the process under discussion. This diagnostic can help you measure your company's performance in terms of the best practices and core insights of other companies—whether or not in the same industry—and pinpoint areas needing improvement.

Our goal for this book is to help you and your managers learn to recognize, analyze, and adapt best-practice insights.

> Arthur Andersen has designed an exclusive
> Best Practices Web site
> (www.arthurandersen.com/bestpractices) where
> readers can go for free additional diagnostic
> assistance and information.

CHAPTER 1

THE LANGUAGE OF PROCESS

NEW INSIGHTS BEYOND BENCHMARKING

Mobil Oil might never have found a way to provide the fast, friendly, consistent, and knowledgeable service its customers wanted if it hadn't been for a racetrack pit crew, a hotel concierge, and a plumbing parts salesman.

What better model existed for getting a car in and out of the service area than that provided by Roger Penske's pit crew? Here was a group of experts who could change tires, check oil levels, fill a gas tank, and clean a windshield in 15 seconds. Of course, Mobil managers weren't aiming to move cars in and out of stations *that* fast, but they did want to know how the Penske team was able to accomplish such a feat.

Mobil managers went to the racetrack and observed the Penske team in action. They took notepads and stopwatches. They listened in on the team members as they communicated with each other through headsets and microphones. Inspired by the Penske team, Mobil devised better training for station attendants and equipped them with Penske-like headsets for easier, faster communication. The Penske-based innovations helped cut more than 30 seconds off the three minutes a customer typically spent filling up at a Mobil station.

What better place for Mobil managers to look for a model of friendly service than Ritz-Carlton hotels? The Ritz-Carlton trains members of its concierge staff to be single-minded in their dedication to meeting customer needs. Mobil managers attended employee training sessions at the Tysons Corner, Virginia, Ritz-Carlton and came away with ideas for developing a culture of customer service that led to major changes in Mobil's hiring and training practices.

Whereas Mobil once considered cash register experience a crucial trait among its applicants, the Ritz-Carlton prompted Mobil managers to change the company's hiring criteria and actively recruit friendly individuals who actually *enjoyed* serving customers. Anybody can learn to run a register, Mobil managers realized, but genuine affability can't be taught.

What better place to find a model for consistent, knowledgeable service than the plumbing parts department at Home Depot? Home Depot tries to win customers for life. The thinking is that a customer, overwhelmed by a single act of kindness and understanding on the part of an employee, will come back again and again. For example, if a customer buys a faucet handle, then accidentally strips the threads, Home Depot will replace it, no questions asked. In fact, most Home Depot associates will offer helpful faucet installation tips.

Inspired by the practices at Home Depot, Mobil instituted its Friendly Serve program, complete with attendants at self-serve islands who offer to check oil and wash windows.

Mobil went through a lot of trouble identifying and benchmarking its best practices. In selecting their own best practices, companies as large as Mobil and as small as a neighborhood drugstore can now rely on a system developed by Arthur Andersen, a knowledge base of more than three thousand best practices covering over a hundred universal business processes. We call it Global Best Practices, and lest *global* seem a bit hyperbolic, consider this: Arthur Andersen has spent more than $30 million to create an ongoing process to tap the expertise of Andersen professionals in 365 offices on every continent and to produce and continuously update what we call our worldwide knowledge base.

In this book, for the first time, we share our thinking and provide a representative sample of some of the best practices stored in our knowledge base, as well as our best ideas for applying these practices to units, departments, and divisions of companies of every size in every industry. At the same time we pass on many of the larger lessons we have learned in establishing and maintaining this enormous collection of organized insights. These best practices are conveyed primarily through stories (case studies). If a picture is worth a thousand words, a good best-practice story is worth a hundred good ideas.

The Arthur Andersen Global Best Practices knowledge base dates back to December 1991, when we at Andersen realized that we already possessed best-practice knowledge that would enable us to add more value to our tens of thousands of clients worldwide. Since 1991 we have been using this best-practice information in our auditing and business consulting services. For example, in the course of our audit work, we typically spent hundreds, in some cases thousands, of hours in a company's offices, plants, and branches studying its business and financial operations. We then compared our observations with generally accepted accounting principles for the company's operations, and that information became the basis for an audit report. But, we realized, if we could also compare the client's operations with specific best practices of other companies, we could more greatly benefit our client.

That opened up whole new worlds to explore. It was all well and good to inform a client company about best practices in its own industry, but we knew that was nothing more than a catch-up game. It could not move the company ahead of the pack, allow it to leapfrog over its competitors. What was really needed was some way of identifying and capturing best practices, not just in terms of a particular industry but *for all industries everywhere.*

We took our stand with the primacy of process. One traditional approach to best practices is to focus on the products or services offered by a particular company as well as on the specific industry trends affecting that company. Automakers tend to look at other automakers, retailers at other retailers, and so on. This industry-centric approach can yield insights, but they are limited. Our experience has taught us that best practices can apply to a variety of industries.

Another traditional way to view best practices is through the lens of functions—research and development, manufacturing, sales, and so on. But a functional approach limits the application of best-practice insights to only part of a process, again limiting their impact. We believe a more practical, realistic way to apply best practices is by universal process—the step-by-step actions taken toward accomplishing an objective. By "universal" we mean that the process is not specific to any particular industry or geographic region; rather, it can be inferred from the close study of many companies in multiple industries and then applied—with appropriate modifications—to any company or industry wherever it is located.

A universal process approach to best practices eliminates the limitations inherent in an industry- or function-based perspective. Because universal process-based best practices are grounded in general rather than industry-specific terms, they are more flexible, more easily changed, and more readily adapted to a variety of business situations. With industry limitations swept away, the process view fosters a larger common playing field and opens the way to the widespread exchange of creative solutions.

We get calls from companies around the world seeking best practices, but unless and until the caller starts speaking the language of process, we cannot be of much help. "Do you have best practice on chicken hatcheries in Australia?" they ask. And we reply, "Wait a minute. What fundamental process are you trying to improve? What part of it? What stakeholder are you trying to serve better?" Then, once the request has been translated into a process-based question, we have to explain that the best-practice solutions for logistics at the chicken hatcheries in Australia may be found at Dell Computer Corporation or Entenmann's Bakery.

Our first step toward creating our process-centered Global Best Practices knowledge base was to identify the key business processes for which we would gather best practices. We wanted to pinpoint not only the universal processes but those that were of special concern to companies at the time. We also worked closely with the International Benchmarking Clearinghouse, a Houston-based nonprofit organization formed in 1992, to develop a classification of the universal processes. We identified 13 primary, or first-level, business processes, along with 260 subprocesses. We think of it as sort of a Standard Industrial Classifications code of business processes.

Most first-level processes define a company's basic operations, such as:

- Understand markets and customers.
- Design products and services.
- Market and sell products and services.
- Produce products and services.
- Deliver products and services.
- Provide customer service.

Supporting these basic operations, management and support processes maximize the value and use of human resources, information and technology, and financial and physical resources, to name a few.

Our second step was to cast the widest possible net for best practices by the major process classifications. We researched the published literature extensively, engaged experts on each key process from around the firm, and sought best-practice information from the ranks of our 50,000 professionals around the world.

In years past, such an all-out information-gathering effort would have been virtually impossible. Most of the valuable knowledge of Arthur Andersen was located in the heads of our individual professionals and on paper in their file cabinets. When a particular problem cropped up with a client, we knew we could consult with those who were serving clients in the same industry. But it was limited by whom we knew and what information was "transferable." At best, it was a hit-or-miss affair.

All that changed when we created our 1.2 gigabyte, 30,000-page Global Best Practices knowledge base. Today, Global Best Practices is one of the hallmarks of Arthur Andersen. It has been used successfully to help thousands of companies worldwide.

This book includes a variety of intriguing and insightful best practices, though they are not, of course, automatically applicable to everyone's circumstances. That would take a tome the size of a library shelf. Instead, we present selected examples of companies that recognize the kernel, the core insight of best practices, and know how to apply it to make a pedestrian process world class. Here are a few cases in point:

1. *Granite Rock.* Managers at Granite Rock, a major supplier of construction materials, gravel, and crushed rock, as well as a general engineering contractor, were unhappy with the processes that customers followed upon entering the gravel quarry, receiving gravel, and completing paperwork for the transactions. Typically, rock was weighed—simply and imprecisely—by the loader-bucketful as it was poured into trucks. This was a very labor- and paperwork-intensive process that took up to 30 minutes and was plagued with errors.

Granite Rock's own best-practice audit of its product delivery process provided it with the inspiration for a whole new system based on a product delivery process already in place at most banks: the automatic teller machine, or ATM. The rocks are heavier than cash, but the concept is the same. Drivers now bring their trucks onto an electronic scale, pass a data card in front of a reader, and punch in the type of rock needed. The trucks then proceed to an overhead aggregate bin where they are automatically filled to the desired weight. The system has cut average truck turnaround time from 24 minutes to seven and allows the quarry to operate 24 hours a day, seven days per week.

2. *GTE*. When the communications giant wanted to streamline and simplify its billing process to reduce input errors, company managers asked, "Who has to handle a huge number of transactions with 100 percent accuracy?" Rather than looking for best practices at another communications company, GTE officials translated their problem into a process and cast their nets farther from the shore. They discovered the Securities Industry Automation Corp. (SIAC), which records anywhere from 400 million to 600 million transactions a day for the New York Stock Exchange.

While there appears to be a great disparity between stock transactions and telephone billing information, the *process* that the SIAC and GTE are working with is identical. The SIAC had discovered how to execute that process efficiently and accurately—precisely the information that GTE needed to turn its billing system around. Needless to say, GTE managers could not simply use a cookie-cutter approach to solving their problems: They had to analyze the performance gaps between the SIAC system and their own, and they had to engage in creative thinking about how to adapt the SIAC's best practice to fit the GTE situation. It turned out that the SIAC had a unique input validation routine that significantly helped GTE.

Similarly, when GTE managers found problems in the company's technical support and repair system, they looked at the Otis Elevator Company, which had developed a nearly foolproof call-center process, using sophisticated databases, for identifying a particular elevator's service record and for initiating repairs by paging the technician responsible for its service. One call set the repair process in motion.

In our practice, we have found that this habit of mind, this ability to seize the core insight of a best practice and then use it as a performance catalyst, is transferable. In this book, we show by precept and example how it is done.

Since creating Global Best Practices, we have often been asked what "global lessons" we have learned in the process, what new insights came to the fore that might provide guidance to managers. After much thought, we recognized that there was indeed a pattern of three common, lasting messages to be found in these thousands of best practices and companies. First on our list:

Constantly Search for a Better Way!

We have found that the companies developing best practices always seek ways to make improvements in their products and services, as well as enhance their relationships with suppliers and customers. Their leaders constantly look up from what they're working on to see what's going on in the world, and they take advantage of what they see. They are on the lookout for all kinds of shifts—major and subtle—and for the changes in product and service preferences that they imply.

We live in a business climate that is so competitive, so unstable and uncertain that we can easily be blindsided. New technologies crop up overnight, it seems, radically changing the terms of competition. The Internet has become to the knowledge economy what electricity was to the industrial economy. New niche competitors appear with products and prices specially tailored to siphon off high-value customers. That means managers must develop their own sophisticated "business radar" and learn to see what's out there beyond the headlights and over the next hill. Anticipating where the next challenge will come from, who their next business partner will be, and who their new customers will be can prepare them for those contingencies.

Not surprisingly, the companies that are most successfully proactive with change are those that have no choice. Organizations in industries like electronics, where product life cycles are 12 to 18 months, don't spend a lot of time resting on their laurels. They are constantly honing their forward radar and searching for new and better ways to improve and speed up their processes. Companies that are in the business of delivering packages the next day, without fail, are constantly scanning the horizon for new developments in dispatch, billing, and inquiry handling. Otherwise, they can't survive. Simply put, those that *have to excel* in a particular process to survive usually demonstrate the best practices in that process.

> **Develop Serious, Positive, Ongoing Relationships with Key Stakeholders to the Business.**

Yes, the second principle we see in action in best-practice companies might appear in any corporate annual report. XYZ, Inc., is "customer focused . . . treats employees as its most important asset . . . partners with suppliers . . . maximizes return to owners . . . and is environmentally responsible." But the leading companies give much more than lip service to these messages.

One manufacturer, AMP, Inc., chooses its suppliers according to their scores on a proprietary index that considers all the costs of doing business with a supplier, not just the product costs but quality, delivery, reliability, and accuracy of shipments and accounting. Those with the highest scores are rewarded with multiyear contracts that truly make them the manufacturer's partners. Under the contract, the supplier agrees to adopt a continuous quality management philosophy, and the manufacturer promises to help the supplier improve its processes with that goal in mind.

Most companies emphasize the value of relationships with customers. But that relationship cannot reach its full potential without commitment to other stakeholders. Unfulfilled, underpaid, overworked frontline employees make for unhappy customers—as well as a growing army of ex-customers. Therefore, the interplay of relationships between customers, suppliers, and employees is a delicate balancing act necessitating constant evaluation and improvement. Moreover, best-practice companies construct strong relationships by increasing the levels of trust and communication between themselves and their stakeholders. This trust has a way of deepening those relationships as it builds upon itself.

Adopt a Strong "Process View" of Your Business.

The third key principle urges that companies view processes as consisting of a series of steps toward a particular objective—customer service, for example, or pollution prevention. The steps one business takes to deliver customer service may differ in superficial ways from those practiced by another, but they are essentially the same. One company may be designing, building, and evaluating prototypes, while another is focused on refining existing merchandise, but both are addressing the same process—the design of products and services. Out of that sameness flows a host of possibilities.

The process view cuts across internal functional boundaries, which means that it allows managers for the first time to see their companies whole, without the impediments of divisions and job titles and particular products. It enables them to map each process, examining each step along the way, precisely targeting where improvements can be made.

We use the term *best practices* throughout this book, but, of course, no single practice works for everyone in any given situation. *Best* is a contextual term. It means "best for *you*"—in the context of your business, your company culture, your use of technology, and your competitive strategies.

The purpose of *Best Practices* is not to find the perfect solution, the best practice that can be lifted intact from a hotel and put to work in a steel plant. That rarely happens. The purpose of *Best Practices* is to disturb you with new ideas and insights. We mean "disturb" in a positive way: All creative ideas and insights have their origin in the minds of people dissatisfied or puzzled by what they encounter in their world. This cognitive dissonance demands a resolution to problems, simple or complex. Sometimes that discovery comes in a sudden illumination; sometimes, over months of trial and error. The Greek mathematician and physicist Archimedes, pondering how to determine whether a crown was pure gold or alloyed with silver, suddenly realized—as he stepped into the public baths—that gold, being more dense than silver, would displace less water. According to legend, in the excitement of his insight, he ran home naked shouting, *"Eureka!"* ("I have found it.")

Perhaps, like Archimedes, you are perplexed by a problem in your business. Maybe you are dissatisfied with your company's current performance or your inability to capture a new market segment. The best practices we describe in this book can trigger that dissatisfaction, causing you to rethink the possible alternatives for your business. In evaluating and improving your basic business processes, you will find much in these best-practice companies to challenge you and the key stakeholders in your business.

Best Practices will, we hope, stimulate your thinking about the universal business processes, relationships, and forces of change that collectively determine your business success.

CHAPTER 2

HEARING IS BELIEVING

THE BEST-PRACTICE AUDIT

In the summer of 2002, Martha Carr opened Coffee Xpress,[1] a wholesale coffee and distribution center in Newark, New Jersey, with three coffeehouses in midtown Manhattan. Offering products such as coffeemakers, espresso machines, and glassware, Coffee Xpress specialized in an extensive line of first-rate coffees and teas from the Far East, Central and South America, and Africa. To serve her coffee shop patrons, Carr contracted with a local bakery to supply sweet rolls, doughnuts, and bagels on a daily basis (except Sundays). Two manufacturers—one located in Michigan and the other in Milan, Italy—supplied medium-priced coffeemakers, which Carr sold at one of the three midtown coffeehouses.

When a good thing happens in New York, of course, people talk. Lots of customers came from uptown and downtown to drink coffee at the midtown Coffee Xpress stores. The wholesale business also did well, selling to restaurants and hotels in the city and in surrounding states as far away as Virginia. As robust as its Arabian espresso, sales at Coffee Xpress brimmed to $3 million in only five years.

Then, however, the bottom line of the business sank to the bottom of Martha Carr's cup. A drought in South America sent coffee prices soaring. Competition from the likes of Zabar's in her own backyard and as far away as Starbucks in Seattle, Washington, and Peet's in Berkeley, California, threatened to turn her stagnating business into lukewarm coffee slush. And the cus-

[1]Coffee Xpress is a composite example combining the actual experiences of many companies.

tomers . . . well, they were just too fickle and unpredictable. In confidence, Carr lamented to her staff that she had no idea how to predict what customers wanted next. One month flavored coffees were all the rage; the next, you couldn't give them away.

Carr tried to set up her own Web page and advertise her products on the Internet, but the site had disappointing results: As few as twenty hits a day brought up nothing more interesting than one user's recipe for making the perfect cup of coffee. A small but enthusiastic group of employees even resorted to door-to-door visits to drum up potential business with restaurant owners, other coffee shop proprietors, even residents in an adjacent building. Although it had moderate success, this effort proved tepid at best.

In frustration, Carr called in her team of salespeople, marketers, wholesalers, distributors, and customer service reps. "It's clear that we can't change this company around with a quick fix or two," she announced. "We ought to do some serious studying of our market, our customers, our sales and distribution channels, and those processes we need to develop in order to survive and prosper."

What Carr was asking for was an audit, but not just in the traditional sense of someone from outside coming in to look at the company's books. The word *audit* has its roots in the Latin *audire* "to hear," more precisely in the form *auditus* meaning "that which is heard." First applied to business in the sixteenth century when it was common practice to have public readings of financial statements that could be "audited" by interested parties, the audit is the first step in understanding the problems that confront the specific business, seeing how those problems can affect *any* business, and then discovering solutions—often in the least expected places.

As we approach the twenty-first century, hearing—both in the sense described above and in the sense of listening carefully to what customers have to say—has never been more crucial. To search for best practices is to study what other companies have accomplished, to adapt their processes to your business situation, and to hear and learn about your customers' experiences with your products and services. In doing so, you should search not only for local wisdom but also for insights from across the street and around the globe. Finally, it is to share this information with people throughout your organization and with your customers and suppliers. Your search for best practices is likely to lead to a refining of products to meet your customers' changing needs and wants. The best way to learn what they need, of course, is to share what you have learned with them.

The decision to audit an organization's processes does not take place in a vacuum. Rather, it is part of a carefully orchestrated undertaking specific to each organization. A best-practice review may lead to some relatively minor adjustments in a company, or it may end in what we call a full organizational transformation.

The review begins by asking the unasked questions of managers, customers, employees, and suppliers, challenging their assumptions about the marketplace as well as future directions it might take. The review studies a client's customers to find out how they define their needs. The review doesn't rely solely on the reports of sales and marketing reps but studies competitors and the degree to which they meet the needs of *their* customers.

The team that examined Coffee Xpress began working closely with Carr and her associates to develop a precise, unambiguous picture of the market environment—what constituted the company's value chain, how the company could act faster and more cheaply, and how it could still give customers exactly what they wanted. The group discussed strategies for improving sales and decided to conduct a thorough study of coffee sales and distribution. This approach required that the team learn everything they could about the entire value chain, which begins with the coffee plantation owner thousands of miles away in Chile and ends with the coffee hound on Eighty-ninth Street and Central Park West who religiously buys three pounds of Mocha Java every two weeks.

Most small companies and a number of large companies, as Carr and her staff came to realize, are not vertically integrated. They have only the slimmest of ideas about who their suppliers are, where the raw materials come from, who can supply those items when the regular suppliers run dry, and how accomplished their competitors have become in integrating those suppliers into their own supply chains. The "market," as the folks at Coffee Xpress had originally conceived of it, consisted solely of customers—either those who walked into one of the coffee shops and ordered a cinnamon roll and a cup of java, or those who mailed in their purchase orders along with a check.

Sensing their error, Carr took pains to point out that the concept of "market" deserves a much broader definition: The market environment includes not only the company's customers but also its suppliers, competitors, and those companies that can furnish substitute products when the coffee industry suffers a devastating drought. And what about those cartels of producers who might decide at any moment to roast their buyers as well as their beans? Mindful of these contingencies, the team began examining the costs of delivering various products, their link to profitability, and the suppliers' place in the delivery chain. Exploring the degree to which employees understand customer needs, the team built an encyclopedic knowledge of Coffee Xpress and developed an instinctive feel for the organization—its strengths and weaknesses.

Then one salesperson in Carr's group brought up yet another matter: Congress would consider the following week a piece of legislation proposing new tariffs to punish some country for offensive international behavior. That country would no doubt retaliate by raising its export duties, forcing companies such as Carr's to raise their prices to consumers. World events could percolate smoothly for months, even years, but then someone would turn up the heat and the whole pot would boil over.

In their study, the team focused on those individual processes and subprocesses currently in place at Coffee Xpress, evaluating each step to determine how the company spent its time and money. First identifying the company's markets and customers in the broadest sense, the team attempted to understand the key forces that motivate customers to purchase coffee products and services, and then segment those customers by appropriate identifying characteristics.

Next, the team examined how Coffee Xpress designed, built, and produced its products. By evaluating the feasibility of these operations, they helped employees at the company learn how to refine existing products or develop new ones to take advantage of segments previously overlooked. After this part of the hearing, the representatives assessed the company's current marketing and sales practices—specifically, its channels of distribution, pricing policies, advertising, sales force deployment, order processing, and strategies to capture customers.

The penultimate stages of the audit process included a scrutiny not only of the company's production capabilities but also of its ability to customize products and services in order to meet customers' current needs and form stable, long-term relationships with them. Once established, those relationships would have to thrive on one-to-one interaction between the company and the customer. "Points of contact"—individual service representatives, salespeople, technicians, and the like—would give the company with its new customer-oriented focus a means of solving problems more quickly. When shared throughout the organization, these service interactions would build cross-functional cooperation.

The company could thus gain a decisive advantage over its competitors.

Finally, the team evaluated how Coffee Xpress could best manage the information that it collected about its customers' purchasing patterns, preferences, and values. Typically, this evaluation often takes the form of suggestions on building a common database to create customer profiles, then tracking the customer's entire experience of buying, receiving, and using a product or service. Through these means the team predicts how successful the company will be if it implements all of the key processes.

In short, the best-practice audit at Coffee Xpress followed these five steps:

1. A multiple-step analysis that identified the problem areas that required attention.
2. A study to find the current flaws in the major business processes and subprocesses that contributed to that problem.
3. Using a strong "process view," a search for possible best practices.
4. A systematic evaluation of each best practice to determine which ones would have the greatest impact.
5. An exploration of ways to incorporate best-practice insights into the processes that affected the problem area.

With a clearer sense of their mission and the advice of their team, Carr and her coworkers identified the problems specific to Coffee Xpress and then began thinking in more general terms to define those problems as they might be experienced by any company in any industry. For example, people at Coffee Xpress had little sense of what their customers wanted beyond that day's cup of coffee. Their problem thus identified, they raised their discussion up a notch to examine the problem in the broader sense of the general process of *understanding markets and customers*. By studying the solutions that companies in other industries as disparate as health care and transportation have implemented for this process, the staff at Coffee Xpress began extrapolating those generic innovations that they could apply to their specific problems.

Carr and her associates scrutinized companies in other industries that had a shrewd and profound understanding of markets and customers. Following the team's suggestions, they began with four companies—Federal Express, Corning, the Lexus division of Toyota, and GE Plastics (all discussed in chapter 4)—whose outstanding results could inspire the Coffee Xpress staff to define more precisely their problems in differentiating their products and services from those offered by large chains.

"I like this idea of looking at ourselves, our suppliers, and our customers from a broad vantage point," said Martha Carr. "By taking this point of view, we can see far and wide, both forests and trees. That's essential in any industry, but if truth be told, we've become too grounded in our thinking."

"How about if we invite another company's representatives to come and watch us and tell us what we're doing wrong or right?" asked Rebecca Joyce, director of marketing at Coffee Xpress. "We need a new pair of eyes, or several pairs of eyes, to see what we and our customers can't see. We could use that kind of vision around here!"

"Although we deal in commodities rather than services like a FedEx," Carr responded, "we are still engaged in the business of satisfying customers as quickly and efficiently as possible. The trick that most great companies seem to have learned is how to partner with their suppliers and customers to incorporate just-in-time principles into their way of doing business.

"Before implementing any of these actions," Carr continued, "we need to examine other companies to see how they come to understand their customers' needs and wants. At present we don't even have a mechanism in place for asking our customers whether or not they like us. And in today's market, that's no way to stay ahead of our competition."

Carr and her associates surveyed various companies for best practices that they could apply to Coffee Xpress. One overarching theme, they agreed, is that the best way to understand customers' needs and wants is to ask them directly. The questionnaire—distributed by hand, fax, modem, or mail—is the most cost-efficient and effective method, but it should have some teeth in it. That is, customers need to know that it is worth their while to write out those comments: They need tangible results in a hurry, some sort of reward or assurance that they will not be taken for granted and their suggestions will not be ignored.

"Why not offer our walk-in customers a doughnut on the house if they will fill out a questionnaire?" one employee ventured. "For our catalog customers who help us with a survey, we could reward them with a free pound of coffee or an extended warranty on the espresso machine they order. And for those big accounts—the hotels and the restaurants—well, there's always free shipping for every fifth order or a discount on orders over a certain amount."

"Those are fine suggestions for prodding customers to respond to our surveys," Carr interjected, "and we can continue to work in that direction. But we also have to go beyond that kind of reward: We need to understand what attracts our customers to us or to our competitors in the first place and what value we can add to the products and services they buy."

"That's right," said Jonathan Wills, head of product development. "But we need to do more than just survey our customers. We need to partner with them to find innovative ways to redesign our products as well as services such as our catering business."

The team agreed with this line of reasoning taken by the Coffee Xpress staff but recognized that their understanding of how to involve customers directly in product design and service delivery was a bit naïve. "Partnering" is much more than just talking to customers, collecting their opinions through surveys, and rewarding them with a doughnut for filling out a questionnaire. True partnering occurs when customers and suppliers participate directly and regularly in the decision-making process. Sometimes a company actually establishes a physical space in its own plants for its partners. It invites them to join staff meetings and to have some access to proprietary information. As discussed in chapter 4, companies such as Varian Associates, Bose Corporation, and Solectron have discovered the value-added benefits of forming constructive partnerships and deeply involving their customers and suppliers in business processes.

After further consultation with the team, the Coffee Xpress staff recognized the value of collaborating with coffee producers abroad. Carr proposed regular trips to plantations in South America and elsewhere where she would work with growers to produce hybrid crops and to perfect the roasting process to meet the needs of her customers. On the home front, the staff agreed to invite both suppliers and customers to visit behind the scenes and help implement changes in such areas as marketing, pricing, service, and delivery.

Equipped with insights from these direct encounters, the Coffee Xpress staff turned their attention to marketing and selling products and services. With the team's guidance they discovered ways to secure their channels of distribution, develop advertising, process orders more efficiently, and build greater loyalty among customers. Studying the likes of Dell Computer Corporation, Lexus, Southwest Airlines, and Allegiance Healthcare Corporation (companies discussed in chapter 5), the Coffee Xpress staff began to see how innovative technology could enhance its marketing and selling processes.

It did not take long for Carr and her colleagues to recognize that the information technology in place at Coffee Xpress was insufficient to achieve the ideals they aspired to. It would take a lot of bytes to segment customers, communicate with suppliers in Central America, and process orders as they thought they should. Although the company could not afford advanced computer networks, Carr began searching for affordable components that could help meet the new challenges her company faced. As she discovered by benchmarking Allegiance Healthcare, other companies already equipped with advanced technology are more than willing to share their capabilities with their business partners.

Continuing its best-practice audit, the Coffee Xpress team determined that its delivery logistics suffered from such problems as unpredictable third-party carriers, poor packaging, and a lack of real-time communication between customers and its New Jersey distribution center. Since all those problems fell under the general category of delivery services, the team directed the Coffee Xpress staff in analyzing the generic process *delivery of products and services*. Next, it helped them identify those best-practice companies that had mastered delivery processes, such as the Campbell Soup Company, Enron Corp., and Cemex (all discussed in chapter 5). Who would have thought that doing something as simple as standardizing the size of delivery pallets could decrease the amount of damage to goods that arrived at a customer's site? But this is exactly what the Coffee Xpress staff gleaned from the best practice that Campbell's had recently put in place at its distribution centers. After implementing similar innovations at its own New Jersey facility, Coffee Xpress would no longer have to ask who spilled the beans.

As a result of delving into such problems in its marketing and delivery processes, the Coffee Xpress staff discovered other areas needing improvement. "We need to give each customer, no matter how large the account, the name and telephone extension of a single contact person here at Coffee Xpress," Carr observed. "This contact should be responsible for seeing that no account is delayed or gets misdirected. Customers will appreciate the personal contact. And while we're on this topic, is each one of us prepared to write personal responses to those customers who respond to our surveys?"

What Carr had pinpointed was a problem in the general area of *providing customer service.* The staff surveyed many companies, such as USAA and the Walt Disney Company (discussed in chapter 7), that had instituted points-of-contact excellence—specific individuals designated to handle any customer inquiry or complaint and empowered financially to provide an immediate solution. Judging from the success of programs that those companies offered their employees, Carr and her colleagues set out to develop similar training for Coffee Xpress employees. Once trained, those staff members would become the contacts that customers could depend on to answer any question—from repairing an espresso maker to shipping 500 pounds of Guatemalan coffee to a hotel in Virginia.

At the conclusion of a best-practice review like the one performed for Coffee Xpress, the team typically assesses the company's ability to manage effectively the information it collects about its customers and suppliers. Because mastering this business process today almost always requires computer technology to build customer profiles, most companies find it necessary to update or invest rather heavily in improving technological capabilities.

In addition, the best-practice company measures customer satisfaction with its products and services. As companies such as Black & Decker, Peapod, and American Express (discussed in chapter 8) have learned, it is often necessary to educate customers themselves in how to operate new products or take full advantage of a company's services. Coffee Xpress, for instance, had received numerous complaints about its espresso machines, but as its Milan supplier had pointed out, creating the perfect cup of espresso is something of an art. Customers *can* be trained in those skills needed to make a better cup of coffee. Accordingly, Carr began making arrangements for her Milan supplier to visit the New York stores and conduct espresso training sessions free to all customers. What better way to ensure customer loyalty?

As the Coffee Xpress example illustrates, the best-practice audit is designed to analyze all of a company's current processes and identify where improvements can be made. Whether a company deals in coffees, cars, or computers, it can learn by listening to the success stories of best-practice companies in all industries and locales. What's working and what's not working for tens of thousands of companies and individuals forms the base knowledge upon which the Arthur Andersen Best-Practice audit is built. In today's complex business environment, we are increasingly persuaded that hearing—not seeing—is key to believing in the best your company can be.

The balance of this book has been organized by the major business processes that support delivering excellence in customer relationships. On the next page is a schematic depiction of the major processes, subprocesses, and chapter references.

This process scheme focuses on achieving excellence in relationships with customers, a major stakeholder of any business. Other stakeholder relationships include those that exist between companies and their employees, suppliers, owners, and the communities they serve.

EXCELLENCE IN CUSTOMER RELATIONSHIPS

PROCESSES FOR IDENTIFYING, DEVELOPING, AND RETAINING CUSTOMERS

Understand Markets and Customers	Involve Customers in the Design of Products and Services	Market and Sell Products and Services	Involve Customers in the Delivery of Products and Services	Provide Customer Service	Manage Customer Information
(Chapter 3)	*(Chapter 4)*	*(Chapter 5)*	*(Chapter 6)*	*(Chapter 7)*	*(Chapter 8)*

SUBPROCESSES

Understand Markets and Customers	Involve Customers in the Design of Products and Services	Market and Sell Products and Services	Involve Customers in the Delivery of Products and Services	Provide Customer Service	Manage Customer Information
Understand the Market Environment	Develop New Concepts and Plans for Products and Services	Secure Channels of Distribution	Offer Broad Delivery Options to Become the "Supplier of Choice"	Establish "Points-of-Contact" Excellence	Build Customer Profiles
Understand Customers' Wants and Needs	Design, Build, and Evaluate Prototypes	Establish Pricing	Use Delivery Customization to Attract and Retain Core Customers	Build Cross-Functional "Points-of-Contact" Cooperation	Establish Service Information
Segment Customers	Refine and Customize Products or Services, Then Test Their Effectiveness	Develop Advertising and Promotion Strategies	Identify Customers' Delivery Needs	Train Employees to Improve Customers' Expectations for Products and Services	Measure Customer Performance and Satisfaction
		Develop and Deploy a Sales Force	Develop Distribution Capability		
		Process Orders			
		Develop Customers			

HITTING A MOVING TARGET

How to Understand Markets and Customers

SUBPROCESSES

UNDERSTAND THE MARKET ENVIRONMENT
UNDERSTAND CUSTOMERS' WANTS AND NEEDS
SEGMENT CUSTOMERS

BEST-PRACTICE COMPANIES

FEDERAL EXPRESS
CORNING
LEXUS DIVISION OF TOYOTA MOTORS
DICKENS DATA SYSTEMS
CONTINENTAL AIRLINES
APPALACHIAN WILDWATERS
FINGERHUT
UNITED AIRLINES
AMERICAN EXPRESS

Business history is replete with companies that failed or faltered because they didn't adequately understand, or were insensitive to, the ever-changing needs of their customers. It is also replete with companies so prescient that they were able to create markets where none existed before and capture customers whose needs changed once those companies came into existence. The lesson is clear: Companies that fail to adapt to changes elsewhere in their industries' value chains are often blindsided by competitors who react to those changes.

Peering into the future is difficult under any circumstances. Short of wizardry and crystal-ball gazing, most managers need to establish formal processes to monitor their company's external environment and customers. A deep understanding of markets, customers, products, and processes becomes vital to the creation of customer value and strategic advantage. Best-practice companies recognize that leveraging knowledge—using existing knowledge about customers to create a keener awareness of market trends— makes good business sense. While these suggestions may sometimes appear to be basic in nature, we believe they underscore timeless and inescapable fundamentals of business.

After completing the initial audit of the company's processes, managers should turn their attention to analyzing the market and better understanding customer needs and wants. In order to gain this knowledge, managers should undertake three distinct subprocesses in sequential order: First, understand the marketplace itself, constantly studying and evaluating the value chain; second, diagnose their customers' needs, including their demands for certain products or services and their desire to solve business problems; third, segment their customers by using a framework constructed from empirical evidence they have collected from customer surveys and other means.

One clear example of understanding the marketplace is Federal Express, the overnight express transportation company that has helped next-day delivery become a fact of modern business life.

Under the direction of founder and CEO Fred Smith, FedEx has made peering into the future practically a science. As far back as 1971, when Smith created the company, the fledgling industry would have starved to death if he had not persuaded the Civil Aeronautics Board (CAB) to change some of the regulations that it had instituted 35 years earlier. Largely at his prompting, the CAB in 1972 changed the restrictions on cargo weight limits, thereby enabling Smith to proceed with plans to launch his Falcon jets.

FedEx arrived precisely at the time that businesses in the United States were catching on to the Japanese concept of just-in-time (JIT) inventory. Why build, support, and maintain warehouses when, according to JIT logic, a company could effectively control the supply and delivery of essential parts and raw materials by having on hand only what it needed to get the job done? Smith saw this change in logistics coming and set his company up to take full advantage of it.

As a result, FedEx built a reputation as the first company to offer overnight delivery practically anywhere in the United States. In 1992, chiefly as a response to customers' distribution problems, FedEx developed its Global Network, a "flying warehouse" that enables a customer to ship products and parts to arrive just at the moment they are needed rather than storing them and incurring inventory costs. National Semiconductor, for example, uses the Global Network to ship computer chips made in Singapore to the West Coast of the United States overnight. Taking advantage of

FedEx's computerized logistics and electronic data interchange (EDI) capabilities, National Semiconductor has reduced its Southeast Asian warehouses from 17 to one.

The changing needs of the market showed Smith and his colleagues at FedEx that "virtual warehousing" was more than just a trend; it was quickly becoming a way of business life. The company now operates other express distribution centers around the world described as more like automatic teller machines than safe-deposit boxes. Those centers offer worldwide connectivity and competitive distribution.

Keeping track of government regulations has been a key component in FedEx's growth and success. Smith and his company recognized that the deregulation of the airline industry in the late 1970s, for instance, would spur U.S. businesses to become more efficient by taking advantage of emerging logistics technology. FedEx now partners with many of its largest customers such as catalog giant L. L. Bean by granting customer service reps access to FedEx's internal COSMOS (computers, operations, and service master online system) for tracking deliveries, down to the details of when the package was delivered and who signed for it.

No company can claim an understanding of the market if it avoids studying demographic and economic trends. At FedEx eyes are always trained on future growth patterns and shifts in economic conditions. In the early 1990s, for example, FedEx began developing a regional express delivery system called AsiaOne. After acquiring Flying Tigers Airlines in 1989 and building a major transportation hub at Subic Bay, the company solidified its position in the Pacific Rim. Now in this center of immense population and economic growth, FedEx has established a presence in every major city from Tokyo and Seoul to Hong Kong and Kuala Lumpur.

Its VirtualOrder service has given FedEx yet more advantages over its competitors. Introduced in 1996, this Internet-based order and fulfillment aid allows customers to search a merchant's catalog electronically for products, check pricing information, and integrate the ordering of products with their delivery to over 200 countries. Electronic commerce (or e-commerce) continues to be an essential ingredient in any company's attempt to leverage knowledge about its markets and customers.

"The nature of commerce is going to change over the next decade," says Sharanjit Singh, FedEx's marketing analysis director. "People want us to make the process of shipping painless for them. FedEx is finding more ways to integrate our systems with those of our customers, providing solutions that save them money, shorten the supply chain, and help them find new customers."

FedEx has leveraged its knowledge of markets and customers to create new services such as its AsiaOne program. Faster innovation of new products is one of the major payoffs that a company experiences by developing this depth of knowledge. The cost a company incurs in conducting a best-practice audit and transforming its processes can often be repaid many times over by savings realized in more rapid research and development of new products. As the subsequent examples illustrate, best-practice companies reach out to both suppliers and customers to gather as much useful knowledge as possible about their market environments.

Subprocess 1
Understand the Market Environment

Achieving an understanding of the market includes gathering information about a company's customers, suppliers, and competitors, other industries, and any relevant aspects of society and government that may have an impact on its business. This information is gleaned from external sources (industry and trade association statistics, government and financial reports, patent filings, academic and trade literature, and so on) as well as from internal sources (reports from the company's sales force or customer service representatives, and so forth). Whatever the source, managers should continually study the entire value chain—from the suppliers' capabilities to competitors' actions, to changes in the distribution channels, to subtle changes in end users' behaviors. This prepares their company to react to—or even anticipate—changes faster than competitors.

Some companies, as Martha Carr and her staff came to realize, are not as vertically integrated with their suppliers as they could be. They may have only a limited sense of where their raw materials come from, who can supply those items when the regular suppliers run dry, and how accomplished their competitors have become in integrating those same suppliers into their own supply chains. The "market," as the folks at Coffee Xpress had originally conceived of it, consisted solely of customers—either those who walked into one of the coffee shops and ordered a cinnamon roll and a cup of java or those who mailed in their purchase orders along with a check. Complete vertical integration along its supply chain, however, might require that Carr or others from Coffee Xpress meet more frequently with suppliers—both coffee plantation owners and manufacturers of various coffee appliances.

Links to suppliers represent only a minor portion of a company's total value chain. At Coffee Xpress the value chain includes not only the intellectual capital that Carr and her employees bring but also the company infrastructure supporting them. As previously discussed in the best-practice audit of chapter 2, this infrastructure includes such elements as marketing, sales, service, advertising, procurement, and delivery.

A systematic analysis of this entire value chain makes managers more sensitive to current threats from competitors and future trends in the marketplace. The analysis can identify openings for expanding the business, developing new customers, and increasing profits. In addition to the basic study of economic and regulatory events, best-practice companies such as Corning and Lexus study the capabilities and innovations of their suppliers, particularly those developing new sources of raw materials and using improved technology to develop component parts. Savvy companies also scrutinize what their competition is doing, as well as noncompeting companies that can provide substitute or complementary products and services.

This industry analysis needs to go beyond merely identifying key players in the marketplace. It must *profile* them, specifying their relative size and growth rates, evaluating their strengths and weaknesses, and studying key events and alliances in their value chains. Simply reading about the merger of two banks or the construction of a new automobile plant can reveal significant developments beyond a mere increase in capacity output.

The market analysis is, of course, never complete. Conditions and customers change too fast for anyone to relax under the false impression that everything to be learned is already in the database. Smart managers know that they not only have to stay vigilant but must also share their findings with company employees, suppliers, and customers. And sometimes that information must even be shared with competitors, as the recent alliance between Microsoft and Apple Computers suggests.

CORNING, INCORPORATED

Although Corning is best known for its Pyrex and other consumer cookware brands, three-quarters of its products are actually used by other companies for inclusion in *their* products. As the first company to enclose Thomas Alva Edison's filament in glass to create the prototype of the modern light bulb, Corning has truly changed with the times. Much of its current work as a supplier to different global manufacturers comes in the high-tech arena, including the growth fields of optical fiber, photonics, and information display.

Corning has worked out a process for better understanding of its customers and their markets. Several of its major processes—event and technology roadmapping, project portfolio management, innovation project management, and customer and market understanding—optimize the creation of ideas and commercialize them for profitable growth.

Event mapping helps Corning better understand the political and other broad-sweeping events shaping the world of tomorrow. The company can thereby envision and plan how to participate in them. In conjunction with event mapping, technology roadmapping focuses on the future *specific* needs of customers and anticipates market trends, thus enabling Corning scientists to best deliver new products and processes when customers need them. Combined, these two processes link innovation to the marketplace.

Charlie Craig, director of process management in science and technology, explains that Corning seeks to understand its customer's total business environment, including the speed of the industry, principal technologies, and legislative and competitive restrictions. The company establishes a cross-functional team comprising experts from marketing, technology, and manufacturing to develop event maps with customers and other industry leaders. Co-development of this information is an essential learning and information-sharing process capable of evolving a complete picture of the product environment.

For example, Corning uses roadmapping to help manufacturers of automotive pollution control devices meet stringent industrial and legislative requirements. The company tracks industrial developments and government reforms, projects events such as compliance dates and increasingly strict emissions standards, and works with its global customers to deliver the technology, cost analysis, and products they need. These include ceramic parts coated with precious metals, the primary components of pollution control devices used in many automobiles, trucks, and buses.

Collaborating with its customers in other areas, Corning supplies materials used in semiconductors and integrated circuits. The company again uses roadmapping to help customers forecast technology and market requirements as they might change over the next five years. These projections prove critical to Corning's ability to improve the materials it manufactures for high-tech circuits—some of which are less than a human hair in width—and to create new capabilities as the next generation of semiconductor technology unfolds.

Once roadmapping is complete, a team translates its projections into a strategy and technology plan geared to deliver the exact product a customer needs. As the environment and the customer's needs change, Corning makes necessary modifications to strategy and product development, always in collaboration with the customer.

After a project is launched, Corning guides it through its innovation cycle. This is a five-stage process: (1) idea generation, (2) concept testing, (3) reduction to practice, (4) scale-up, and (5) commercialization. Constant monitoring of market trends and customer needs takes place as the idea matures through the innovation cycle, thus ensuring that the concept will satisfy the customer's requirements. Managers gather information from market, technology, and manufacturing representatives to ensure that commercial technology and cost requirements are updated at each stage of the project.

Often an original equipment manufacturer of high-technology projects, Corning finds this five-stage process useful in understanding the requirements and time restraints that customers are planning for in development of *their own* products—those into which Corning's products will be integrated. Sharing a common innovation framework and language, Corning and its customers can achieve breakthrough innovations.

"The interesting thing about this approach is that you can actually work with customers at different points in the value chain to define the future," Craig explains. "Some of these customers depend on you for the innovations; others are the lead users or innovators themselves and want to work *with* you." This is particularly important for Corning in the photonics arena, the liquid crystal display substrate market, and in many of its advanced materials businesses worldwide. To promote the customer-innovation connection, Corning has four research and development laboratories strategically situated in the United States, Europe, Japan, and Russia.

"You have to be able to anticipate what's going to happen five or ten years from now and what that's going to mean to your technology development program," says Craig. "Some of those near-term needs will be reasonably definable, but some of the long-term items will be more blue-sky when technology and market discontinuities converge. Our goal is to be not just a supplier but also a partner to our customers."

LEXUS DIVISION OF TOYOTA MOTOR CORPORATION

In the 1970s, the Toyota Motor Corporation wrote the book on just-in-time manufacturing, and the company's Lexus division is the beneficiary of all the efficiency that comes with such a clear understanding of the market and its value chain. Like its parent Toyota, the Lexus division is a huge operation comprising hundreds of suppliers who make such items as brake parts, steering assemblies, and gaskets for every automobile that rolls off the line in Japan and into a Lexus showroom in North America. Without a clear understanding of its customers, the company would never be able to meet their demands and stay ahead of its competitors in the luxury car market.

Yet as Steven Sturm, corporate marketing manager of Lexus, points out, "Luxury cars tend to offer customers only a handful of options. After all, luxury cars come fully equipped: What would be an option on a Toyota Corolla, such as power windows, comes as standard equipment on an LS [Lexus] 400. Ordering an ES 300, a customer can request a sunroof, CD player, chrome wheels, cellular telephone, and the like, but otherwise a luxury car owner expects the car to come loaded."

Special orders, of course, take longer to produce. Depending on when a customer places an order, the request for a red Lexus with a sunroof, special leather interior, and wheel locks might take only a few hours if the company's integrated computer system finds a match at a neighboring dealership. Or the request could take a month or longer if the automobile is not available in the United States.

"It's not unusual for us to ship a car from one dealer to another to meet a customer's needs," says Sturm, "or to reroute it from its arrival in Long Beach, California, to Tampa, Florida, for example." Lexus considers this fulfillment of special orders a key element in its total picture of the market. Achieving prompt fulfillment, just-in-time manufacturing has helped make Toyota one of the most efficient automobile operations in the world.

Although just-in-time manufacturing has been criticized for

placing a company at risk when one link in the chain breaks, Toyota, and by extension Lexus, has managed to react quickly to potential crises. Such an event occurred in February 1997 when the Aisin Seiki plant near Nagoya, Japan, caught fire and suffered extensive damage. A major supplier of brake and clutch parts to Toyota, which owns approximately one-fourth of the supplier, the Aisin Seiki Company is such an essential part of the automobile manufacturer's supply chain that the catastrophe caused shock waves throughout the system. For about a week, 17 of Toyota's 18 automobile plants in Japan had to cease operation. Most companies with this degree of dependence on a single-source supplier would be shut down much longer than that. But other suppliers in the Toyota-Lexus chain stepped in. "Several of the others that work with Toyota," says Sturm, "helped make up for this loss of a critical part and got us back in gear literally in days."

The resilience that Lexus demonstrated in what could have been a shattering event is a trademark of a best-practice company with a full view of its value chain. The Lexus division invests in both external and internal research to determine what trends are influencing the market—and where it is heading. Like all drivers, Lexus owners want to get from point A to point B, but they also expect a product with no faults and plenty of creature comforts. Lexus has made a best practice of matching up those expectations with the various elements in its supply chain that can deliver dreams at practically a moment's notice.

As a relatively late arrival in the U.S. luxury car market, Lexus has learned to keep refining its strategy to capture luxury customers and increase its market share. Debuting in 1989, the company priced its luxury models below those of the other major automobile manufacturers such as Cadillac, Lincoln, Mercedes-Benz, and BMW. Those other companies, however, have responded by redesigning or cutting prices on some models. The need to understand the market, therefore, has taken on new significance for Lexus, which plans to come out with new models of its own.

Like so many others, the automobile industry demands that companies continually revise and improve products. As Sturm puts it, "The bar keeps moving up, so what you did yesterday is not necessarily going to work today, much less tomorrow. You've got to keep setting new standards." Because the market is always changing, Lexus recognizes the importance of training *all* its associates in the intricacies of every new model the company introduces. This means a new training and certification program at least once a year to help associates increase their knowledge of the products and improve their customer relations skills. As a best-practice company, Lexus has greatly benefited from sharing its understanding of the value chain with employees, suppliers, and customers.

Subprocess 2
Understand Customers' Wants and Needs

How many companies can distinguish the first-time buyer from the regulars, enumerate the benefits a customer receives from a product or service, and take into account critical incidents that shape that customer's perception of the company? Many companies today have neither the means nor the incentive to study their customers this deeply, although all would benefit from such an inquiry. Profiling customers and becoming sensitive to their needs can not only help a company develop products and services more valuable to those customers but also enable the company to become a market leader.

The subprocess *understanding customers' wants and needs* can be channeled into three areas: assessing "value-in-use" benefits, measuring critical incidents, and analyzing customers' purchasing patterns that reflect expectations and responses. Best-practice companies use a variety of external and internal sources for collecting information relevant to those three areas.

Value-in-use benefits include, first, an understanding of the immediate gratification a customer derives from a product. If someone orders a new computer, for instance, he or she expects it to arrive in good condition, be easy to set up, and start running immediately. Only later, perhaps, will that customer be concerned with warranties or service needs. A best-practice company such as Dell Computer Corporation is always prepared to meet those needs when they arise—precisely because they *know* what their customers' needs are.

The customer's overall experience with the product or service offers numerous occasions for contacting the company. From the moment a customer selects a product to the instant he or she requests a delivery or service call, the experience cycle shapes that customer's perception of the company and its products. Any one of those contacts—be it a very good or very bad incident—is critical in determining whether the customer becomes a loyal or a disgruntled consumer.

The expectations and criteria for selecting a product are different for first-time buyers than they are for repeat buyers, who most likely have been treated well in the past. A company can help ensure that customers remain loyal by offering them consistent pricing and availability, individual attention, and a sense of shared values. As Dickens Data Systems (discussed below) illustrates, customers appreciate and profit from the degree of collaboration they receive in solving hardware and software problems when they arise. Similarly, as Continental Airlines (also discussed below) has learned, it cannot operate a customer service function that merely seeks to resolve complaints; rather, customer service has become intimately connected to Continental's effort to understand its customers' needs, such as low-salt or reduced-calorie meals.

Understanding customers' needs and wants therefore involves much more than complaint resolution. Done properly, this subprocess includes analyzing the entire customer purchase cycle. A company constantly seeks information from and about its customers, then collaborates with them to give them what they want.

DICKENS DATA SYSTEMS, INC.

Based in Roswell, Georgia, a major high-tech region near Atlanta, Dickens Data Systems is a premier partner of IBM and nationwide systems integrator and distributor of IBM's mid-range systems and software. Its diverse customers specialize in such industries as health care, accounting, wholesale distribution, and government, and include a number of end users. Founded in 1981, Dickens Data has "never been unprofitable," according to chief financial officer Warren Turner. From the looks of its recent improvements in understanding its customers' wants and needs, the company is building its future on creating and maintaining the highest quality in both its products and services and its customer relationships.

Like many companies, Dickens Data surveys its customers. Unlike most of those companies, it does so *every three months*. Although its average customer does at least $75,000 worth of business quarterly, Dickens Data surveys anyone who makes just $1,000 worth of purchases during that time. Within two days of receiving a negative response on a survey, a customer advocate calls that customer to resolve the problem. Furthermore, all Dickens Data executives review every survey and share this information throughout the company.

But the process does not stop there: CEO Gordon Dickens responds to every customer who returns a survey by sending a personally signed letter and a gift of appreciation. "You don't have to spend a lot of money on a quality program," says Dickens, "just start sending your customers one letter a quarter asking them whether they like you or not. For the cost of one stamp per customer, plus your stationery and letterhead, you'd be amazed at what you can learn."

Since its quarterly survey was established in 1994, Dickens says, company sales have increased from about $25 million to over $300 million. He estimates that nearly 20 percent of this increase can be attributed directly to the company's extensive surveying. Over the first four years, only one customer requested to be removed from the polling lists.

Thanks in part to its surveys, Dickens Data has developed a deep understanding of its customers and their needs. In an effort to broaden that awareness, company executives and directors attend IBM partner conferences and trade shows several times a year. Here they facilitate face-to-face meetings between customers and vendors, increasing their understanding of those customers' needs.

Segmented by industry, "solution providers" form the single largest group of customers for Dickens Data. The company collaborates with each group of solution providers to create value-added packages of hardware and software tailored to each major industry. Thus, a medically-oriented provider might construct a set of solutions geared to answer problems faced by hospitals, HMOs, or clinics—such as patient tracking, appointments, billing, and drug therapies. An accounting firm might instead need access to comparative data from its various clients, whereas a wholesale distributor might require specific information on loading and shipping requirements for its customers.

These surveys provide Dickens Data employees with valuable information about how customers value their performance. Based on the response, company management calculates a "net satisfaction index" (NSI), rating each employee and each department according to customer perception. "Everyone here will work with any customer to fix a problem," says Kim Massa, manager of quality and customer satisfaction at Dickens Data.

Moreover, employees rate *one another*, using a similar survey to gauge a job well done. The company uses results from these internal and external reports to determine significant portions of employees' compensation and bonuses. "Without the quality program, there was a lot of employee and customer dissatisfaction," says Gordon Dickens. "But once we were able to put together programs to address those issues, the NSI rose, and morale among our employees improved dramatically."

CONTINENTAL AIRLINES

For years it was joked that the best-kept secret of Continental Airlines was the telephone number of Customer Relations. The company, which went through ten presidents in ten years, consistently ranked at the bottom of the airline industry in the services it provided to its customers, including the way it handled their complaints. The airline's performance record so demoralized some employees that they refused to wear the company logo on their uniforms.

Lately, however, the company has made dramatic improvements. Under CEO Gordon Bethune, Continental became the first company in the airline industry to install a 24-hour, toll-free number (1-800-WE CARE-2) to help customers resolve problems related to lost luggage, reservations, in-flight meals, entertainment, and special services for the disabled. Since Continental began this service in 1995, many other airlines have copied it.

A small change that signaled a major shift in Continental's attitude toward its customers came when former head of customer service P. J. Robinette changed the name of the department to Customer Care. Whatever a customer requests—"I'd rather have mustard than mayonnaise on my sandwich" or "I'd like more choice in the classical music offerings"—that message is now heard throughout the company.

As noted by Judith Mensinger, Continental's current director of Customer Care, the 800 number accounts for 70 percent of the thousands of customer contacts her department handles each week. "Our objective," she explains, "is to resolve customer service requests at the first point of contact, usually in the initial phone call."

At the end of each month, the Customer Care department tabulates all comments received through its toll-free number. Mensinger and her staff categorize those suggestions and calculate the percentages for each area of concern. This report is forwarded to every division in the company so that everyone sees what customers like and dislike about Continental's service. In addition, the airline now surveys customers through postage-paid comment cards available in its in-flight magazine, through telephone interviews, and by means of its Internet site.

After soliciting comments from 4,500 of its frequent fliers, for example, Continental discovered that most customers were concerned about the kind of food being served on board long-distance flights. Reflecting health-conscious attitudes prevalent in today's society, these passengers asked the airline to revise its in-flight menus. Continental responded with healthier, lighter fare; now customers can request low-salt or reduced-calorie meals rather than the standard menu. And for those who want exotic drinks, Continental has added Pete's Wicked Ale and Brothers Foglifter Gourmet Coffee to its cart.

Also in response to customers' requests, the airline has improved other in-flight services. At one time Continental had removed all packages of aspirin in order to save $10,000—a frugal step that left many customers disgruntled—but now passengers need no longer worry about finding a remedy for in-flight headaches. As a result of customer demand, the airline has restocked its medicine cabinet.

Continental further established a more efficient automated system for resolving customers' problems and enlarged its customer service staff. After fielding suggestions from its customers, Continental replaced its automated call distributor system with a new one provided by Rockwell Industries. Since the new system evenly distributes calls throughout Continental's five reservations centers, customers never need to wait long for a ticket agent.

In short, Continental has made outstanding progress in turning around a dreadful relationship with its customers by listening carefully to what they have to say, taking their suggestions seriously, and providing them with additional means for making those complaints heard. No customer wants to stuff a letter of complaint into a bottle in hopes it will wash up on the shore of the appropriate corporate department. With its surveys and customer care program, Continental has made sure that won't happen. And unlike many other airlines and the Department of Transportation, which respond with form letters, Continental employees answer each customer's letter individually.

APPALACHIAN WILDWATERS, INC.

Imre Szilagyi, president and CEO of Appalachian Wildwaters, Inc., in Rowlesburg, West Virginia, considers himself a problem solver. Trained as a mathematician at the Ohio State University, Szilagyi developed a passion for kayaking and white-water rafting. In 1972, he founded a small rafting company that offered tourists and weekend athletes a ride down the New River in West Virginia. Through effectively tracking and responding to customer needs, Szilagyi has turned his company into one of the premier rafting outfits in the United States.

Back in 1972, Appalachian Wildwaters enjoyed an almost unchallenged position on the river (it had only one competitor). Within five years, however, a dozen rafting companies had brought in their boats and siphoned off many of Appalachian Wildwaters' customers. In addition to seeing more competitors, Szilagyi saw fewer smiles on his customers' faces. His employees were growing bored, manifested in their sloppy dress and hygiene. On several downriver voyages, Szilagyi heard the guides using coarse language, not the sort of thing he wanted to become a trademark of his rafting company.

After pleading, begging, cajoling, and bribing, Szilagyi got serious with his employees. He proposed that the guides give each customer a short questionnaire to complete during the 25-minute bus ride back to base camp. Every guest would evaluate the entire white-water experience—everything from safety measures on board the raft to the guide's expertise and courtesy. At least half of the questions were open-ended: What would guests like to see the company do differently? What did they particularly like or dislike?

Guides at first resisted the surveys, complaining that it was their prerogative to judge the customers' abilities, not vice versa. "Those comment cards changed the culture of our organization," Szilagyi explains. "We were guide-oriented, but now we're customer-oriented. That shift of focus represents a sea change for the company."

This change has since rippled through every part of the organization, from the kitchen to the campground. Customers said they didn't like life jackets spotted with mildew or perspiration. (The company bought new ones.) Many disliked sandwiches made with white bread. (The chefs started using whole wheat.) And most wanted cold beer at the end of their downriver voyage. They even went so far as to name the beer: "We want Budweiser!" (And so Bud they got.)

One customer suggested that the company make a videotape of each trip, an idea that became a reality when affordable, handheld cameras came on the market. Tents with waterproof floors and mosquito netting are now standard equipment on every overnight trip. The base camp offers more deck space because customers said they wanted a place to relax. (Smokers got their own deck.) A pool and a hot tub are in the works.

Over time, the survey cards have become a major factor in evaluating employees' behavior as well as determining salaries and bonuses. At the end of each trip, the surveys are sorted. Each guide reads the comments of customers on his or her raft, then shares those comments with other guides. The trip leader reads all the surveys. Depending on the positive feedback from the evaluations, the company awards a bonus of up to $10 per trip to each guide. Although employees initially resisted this system of rewards, they have come to support it as they see the difference it has made in the company's success.

Perhaps the most significant change at the company came as a direct result of the customer surveys. Concerned over prices, customers asked for less expensive, less time-consuming white-water trips. Appalachian Wildwaters responded by creating a new company, USA Raft, with a mission to "keep the thrills but do away with the frills." Beginning further downriver, USA Raft customers still experience the rapids but end their trips sooner, thereby avoiding the expense for lunch and the longer trek back to camp. Applying Appalachian Wildwaters' commitment to customer satisfaction, USA Raft now operates on nine rivers in four states. And the two companies combined are among the largest in the United States in providing white-water experiences.

Thanks to that systematic (and serious) commitment to understanding customers' needs and wants, Appalachian Wildwaters and USA Raft together have left the competition on the sandbars. Because customers can see the company actually incorporating the changes they suggest, they now believe it when the company proclaims its new watchword as "zero disappointments."

And Szilagyi, the mathematician turned whitewater rafter, is still doing what he loves: solving problems.

Subprocess 3
Segment Customers

After surveying customers to determine how they react to products and services, the best-practice company seeks to divide a large, heterogeneous group of customers into smaller units defined by unique needs, purchasing characteristics, or other criteria such as economic and demographic factors. Effective market segmentation requires that the company develop clear strategies about what it hopes to accomplish and a plan of action to improve satisfaction levels, increase profits, and build market share. A good segmentation strategy can accomplish all three goals.

Although not absolutely necessary to this subprocess, information technology has proved a great boon in developing segmentation. Larger companies can now tailor marketing strategies and product offerings to ever smaller segments, often making the direct appeal to a single customer. Just as Varian Associates collaborates with its clients, customizing products to fit individual needs, so other best-practice companies have perfected this subprocess to provide solutions to particular problems or needs of their customers.

Depending on the industry or products involved, successful segmentation can be expensive, not to mention time-consuming and logistically challenging. Its return, however, in terms of satisfied, loyal customers, and increased customer profitability can easily compensate for the initial expense. This is a lesson that best-practice companies such as American Express, Fingerhut, and United Airlines can teach by their example.

FINGERHUT COMPANY, INC.

The second-largest catalog company in the United States, Fingerhut tailors products and services to customers who have difficulty establishing credit with other companies. In a market hit hard by soaring prices for printing and mailing catalogs—witness the demise of that old standby, the Sears, Roebuck catalog, now a collector's item—Fingerhut executives knew that they had to perform major surgery on the company to keep it healthy in the 1980s and 1990s.

Chairman and CEO Ted Deikel directed a major reengineering effort in 1989 as Fingerhut moved out from under the control of the Travelers Company and became an independent organization. Based in Minnetonka, Minnesota, Fingerhut recently moved two large telemarketing facilities to south Florida, primarily to take advantage of a large supply of potential employees who are fluent in Spanish. According to Deikel, Hispanics constituted about 5 percent of Fingerhut's business in 1996, but demographic predictions indicate that this segment of the population will experience dramatic increases in the next three or four decades. In

1996, Fingerhut's Hispanic customer list grew by 33 percent. The company wants to be where the customers will be, hence the appeal of south Florida.

The establishment of these new branches illustrates Fingerhut's determination to appeal to specific segments of its customer base. Understanding the needs and wants of retirees (concentrated in the Tampa/St. Petersburg area), Hispanics (particularly the large population of Cuban exiles in the Miami region), and other major segments of the population becomes a key strategy in satisfying customers. It also helps the company stay ahead of thousands of competitors who every day mail out *their* catalogs to eager customers.

How does Fingerhut keep its finger on the pulse of customers' wants? It conducts surveys—relentlessly. Since 1993, the company has conducted a telephone survey of 200 different customers *each month*. Those who participate in the survey must meet certain criteria: They must have purchased from a Fingerhut catalog within the previous six weeks, made at least one credit payment, and had an opportunity to return an unsatisfactory item. In other words, each person participating in the survey has completed the purchasing cycle: From the time he or she first saw the advertisement, then ordered the item, then began making installment payments, that customer has been a part of the cycle. Only at this finishing point does Fingerhut believe the customer is prepared to give a full response to the satisfaction questionnaire.

Collecting data on its customers has always been a part of the company's philosophy and practice. In the 1960s, with the growth of computers, this data collection became much more systematic, but by the 1990s it became thoroughly incorporated into Fingerhut's vast database of customer profiles, credit histories, and purchasing activity. Since 1993, the company has used this data to construct a trend line called the Lifetime Profitability Analysis, which gives it an enormous advantage over competitors who do not know their customers so well.

The objective is to capture every customer interaction as well as any costs associated with an order or with the customer's decision to return the merchandise. (In this case, the item may have to be refurbished before being resold or replaced entirely.) The company tracks every financial implication of every interaction with a customer, including any credit loss, account allowance, and shipping costs. It measures how much it costs to process a customer's order, to take in a returned item, even to induce a customer to buy a product (for instance, by offering a free gift, a promotional incentive, or an upgrade to a premium product). According to Andy Johnson, senior vice president at Fingerhut, "We use all this information to create an idea of *customer profitability:* We allocate a portion of our fixed overhead to each interaction, and we come out with a pretax profit line at the customer level."

By engaging the customer in this relationship with the company, Fingerhut not only erects an enormous barrier to entry against upstart competitors but also determines which customers it no longer wants to do business with. In short, Fingerhut chooses its customers by researching each one it has had in its 40-year history of providing credit.

Even those who have fallen short in their repayment plans have a chance to regain status as Fingerhut customers. The company keeps track of customers whose credit history includes perhaps as many as four or five good interactions, with prompt repayments, but then for some reason—the loss of a job or a family illness, for instance—those customers fail to complete a payment schedule. Using segmentation criteria to distinguish customers in this group from the truly bad credit risks, Fingerhut's representatives offer the opportunity to reestablish a relationship with the company. Most people are eager to rebuild their credit, and these recaptured customers tend to be good credit risks, despite the reluctance of other creditors even to consider their applications.

Through its sophisticated database information, Fingerhut has turned the extending of credit into something approaching a science. The company forms statistical algorithms to predict response rates as well as credit risks. Those algorithms take into account the length of time a person has been a Fingerhut customer, the number of offers already extended, how many times the customer has made a purchase, the maximum number of days the account has been delinquent, the average payment obligation to Fingerhut, and numerous other factors.

All this information goes into the database, which then determines ever finer slices—or segments—of the market. As Andy Johnson puts it, "Sometimes these algorithms are so powerful that we don't find it economically viable to spend the money to contact customers in order to ask them whether they intend to pay us or not."

Few companies can match Fingerhut in the construction of customer profiles and credit histories, although with the advent of more sophisticated information technology, other companies are bound to follow suit. In terms of segmenting customers and determining which ones make acceptable credit risks, Fingerhut sets the standard for direct marketers and all industries where knowing the customer is essential to success.

UNITED AIRLINES

The employees who own and operate United Airlines know the value of segmenting customers. For several years the company has identified those frequent fliers who accumulate 100,000 miles per year. Its "Adopt a Premier" program, initiated in 1994–95, is a company-wide plan in which United executives and management representatives are each assigned a 100,000-plus traveler to contact with offers of assistance other than just more upgrades on future flights. United has found that such segmentation establishes a stronger bond between the company and its top customers.

"We personally call each Premier and ask what we can do for that customer," explains Bill Byrne, United's director of culture and corporate education. "Most customers respond to our surveys by telling us that they simply want to be treated more personally. They don't just want upgrades; they want respect."

This respect now comes in various ways. A United employee meets a Premier member for lunch, helps him or her get to a gate on time, or simply provides assistance in booking a seat on a particularly crowded flight. The needs vary, but the goal remains the same. "You just do everything possible to make their travel better," explains Patricia O'Brien Saari, an account executive in United's Seattle office.

According to Saari, Premier members account for 52 percent of United's full-fare business in the Seattle area. Each represents over $1,500 of business per week. With these numbers in mind, in 1996 Saari and her coworkers initiated a separate volunteer program called "100,000 Miles of Thanks." Seattle employees from reservation agents to airplane fuelers to baggage handlers wrote letters of gratitude to Premier members inviting them to take advantage of privileges such as a priority waiting list for upgrades and the Premier seating zone available on all flights. Premiers also have their own room at Seattle-Tacoma Airport where they can use business machines.

"We wanted *all* our employees to get involved with contacting customers," explains Saari. "Just a simple thank-you makes the customer feel good and helps employees realize there is a customer out there who cares that they're doing their job. In the end, we had 750 different 100,000-milers contacted by 750 different

United employees." Customer response to the initiative was so positive that United has added the program in other cities.

In addition to these efforts, United has initiated a special benefits program for VIPs who work for corporations that accumulate more than 100,000 miles annually. Three or four members of United's Special Services department greet these VIP customers, help them check in, take care of their baggage, and even run to buy presents for their children before their flights depart. No matter how rushed an individual may be, that kind of effort is likely to be remembered—and rewarded.

AMERICAN EXPRESS CORPORATION

Few industries have undergone the kinds of tumultuous changes that the credit card business has experienced over the last two decades. Consumer debt is now a major economic indicator, and the numbers are soaring. The daily mail continues to offer more and more potential customers an ever-increasing array of credit cards to choose from.

Segmenting customers takes on special significance in this industry, as American Express can testify. Although the American Express and Optima cards form only one side of its multifaceted business, which includes financial and travel services, American Express knows that it has to maintain close relationships with its cardmembers. According to Amy Radin, vice president of rewards development at American Express, the company uses customer surveys to obtain a deeper understanding of its cardmembers' perceptions and needs. Holders of personal cards, gold cards, and platinum cards may be asked similar questions, but the company is primarily interested in discovering how customers as individuals view the company's services and how satisfied they are with them.

American Express has always used traditional criteria to segment customers, such as credit history and income, to help the company determine who is best suited for a particular type of charge or credit card. Those traditional measures, however, are standard for the entire industry. Seeking to distinguish itself from competitors, American Express now goes several steps further to show how it understands and responds to customer needs.

First, the company segments customers according to life stage. Senior members, for example, receive a cardmember values page with their monthly bills; this page advertises discounts on products and services geared to their group. College students, on the other hand, receive a different values page, advertising items such as special airfares, CDs, sports equipment, and the like.

Second, according to Radin, the company is switching from preprinted to laser-printed values pages customized to increasingly narrow segments of customers based on how they use their American Express cards. "In the past there have been about ten offers on a values page, but the customer might have an interest in only two or three," she explains. "When we laser-generate these pages, our goal is to target and model them to give customers all the choices that best suit their needs. If a customer travels frequently, he or she will receive a set of offers (discounts on airfares, hotel rates, luggage, and so forth) that is different from that received by a customer who rarely travels but is a big retail shopper."

The third and most innovative step in this process of segmentation is an American Express program called Custom Extras. The company has a detailed record, of course, of every purchase a customer makes and how often that purchase is made. All this information is maintained in a database that the company can tap to further segment customers according to industry and merchant preferences. These capabilities enable American Express to develop and manage a cost-efficient loyalty program for its merchants as well as rewards and incentives for its customers.

Using sophisticated databases, for example, American Express can now more quickly identify customers who regularly buy shoes at a particular store. Recognizing this pattern in purchases, the company will work with the store's managers to develop discount offers to that specific segment of customers in order to build loyalty to that store.

And where is the best place to get customers involved in this process? The one place American Express knows it always has its customers' attention is the monthly billing statement. Customers can benefit from this segmentation process by receiving special discounts on products they purchase frequently. On its newly redesigned billing statements, American Express now lists discount offers beside certain purchases that the company knows the cardmember will appreciate.

"Custom Extras provides the merchants with a tool to build loyalty with their American Express customers," says Radin. "And it lets us use our statements to deliver the rewards in a personalized way. The shoe customer, for instance, might receive a message like 'Thanks for shopping with us. Next time you come in, we'll give you a $25 discount on your purchase!'"

Yet another component of this segmentation process, the Express Rewards program, takes advantage of existing technology to offer customers special rewards at the point of sale. American Express partners with many merchants by segmenting customers according to the frequency and amount of purchasing they do. When those customers make their next purchases at that merchant's place of business, the transaction will trigger a VIP signal to alert the merchant that loyal customers need to be rewarded. If, for example, a customer who regularly eats at a particular restaurant pays with the American Express card, the waiter will be alerted to the customer's VIP status and can then offer a predetermined reward: "We see you are a regular customer at our restaurant. As a token of our appreciation, your dessert tonight is on us!"

American Express has learned that customer segmentation builds loyalty and leads to better relationships between merchants, customers, and the company that serves them both. According to Radin, "We're providing solutions to the challenge that both our merchants and we at American Express have: How do you build loyalty with specific customers? This is one of the primary objectives of customer segmentation. With our technology we are now in a position to increase both value and relevance for *all* our cardmembers."

What company would not prefer to *choose* the customers it does business with? Most managers, however, only dream about what companies such as Fingerhut, United Airlines, and American Express have accomplished. Those companies have built best practices in the segmentation of customers and are so good at it that they can pinpoint the customers they want to work with. Once that choice is made, the company can decide how best to tailor products and services to meet the needs of those customers. Systematically implemented, the subprocess of segmentation can enable a company to build loyal relationships with the best customers possible.

From the examples of the nine companies described throughout this chapter, we can infer a general process of best-practice methods for understanding markets and customers. We call this the Best-Practice Agenda.

BEST-PRACTICE AGENDA

Understand that the market is more than just the customer. In its broadest sense, the market environment includes the company's supply chain and merchant partners as well as intermediary customers and end users. As demonstrated by Federal Express with its flying warehouses and Lexus with its quick response to a fire at a supplier's facility, a company's understanding of government regulations, trends in consumer purchasing, and unpredictable events can dramatically affect its production and relationship with customers.

Systematically create an image of the company's value chain, from suppliers to end users. Prominently displayed, this diagram serves to inform all employees how they fit into the market environment as well as how other stakeholders with whom *they* deal (customers, suppliers, and so forth) also fit into the market environment.

Survey your customers frequently, systematically, directly, and personally. Review the surveys and then share them with the people in your organization who need to know what those customers have to say. The example of Gordon Dickens, CEO of Dickens Data, who responds personally to every survey, should provide the norm for executive behavior. If you don't have the time to respond personally, make sure someone in your company does.

Revise your products or services as customers request or tell them why they can't have it their way. Promote the new version and resurvey customers to assess their satisfaction. Imre Szilagyi, CEO of Appalachian Wildwaters, surveys every customer on his white-water trips and requires every guide to read and respond to those comments. Requests for new products and services have led to expanded offerings and even a second company, USA Raft.

Segment customers so that you can meet demands more directly and profitably. Establish the criteria by which customers should be grouped (by age, income, credit history, purchases, demographic factors, and so forth), then offer products and services tailored to those segments. When appropriate, partner with merchants and suppliers to create greater value for customers, as American Express does.

Top Ten Best-Practice Diagnostic Questions

1. Can you describe in detail all the major suppliers in your company's value chain and list substitute suppliers who could provide raw materials and component parts in an emergency? Do you need a week's review to do so? (You won't have a week if a fire destroys a supplier's production plant.)

2. How often do you survey your customers? Once a month? Once a year? Once a millennium?

3. Which customers do you choose to survey? Only those who call you first?

4. How good is your process for responding to customer concerns expressed in surveys?

5. What quick, tangible rewards do you offer customers who take the time to complete one of your surveys or requests for information?

6. What external sources other than surveys do you typically use to gather information about your customers? About competitors? About suppliers? About trends in the marketplace?

7. What other internal sources do you use to collect this information?

8. List five (or more) segmentations that your company currently uses. Can you explain succinctly the benefits it realizes from grouping customers as it does?

9. Name a product or service your company provides that has

come about as a result of a customer request or survey and has since improved your overall profitability.

10. Does your company have a process for customers to evaluate your employees and departments? Is it similar to the Net Satisfaction Index that Dickens Data Systems has developed? Do you support cross-functional teams to analyze customer needs and fulfill them?

CHAPTER 4

"NOT EMPLOYEES ONLY"

How to Involve Customers in the Design of Products and Services

SUBPROCESSES

DEVELOP NEW CONCEPTS AND PLANS FOR PRODUCTS AND SERVICES

DESIGN, BUILD, AND EVALUATE PROTOTYPES

REFINE AND CUSTOMIZE PRODUCTS OR SERVICES, THEN TEST THEIR EFFECTIVENESS

BEST-PRACTICE COMPANIES

BLACK & DECKER

SOLECTRON

VARIAN ASSOCIATES

GE PLASTICS

BOSE (JIT II)

AMP

THE WALT DISNEY COMPANY

One of the most popular products that tool manufacturer Black & Decker has developed in the past several years is its SnakeLight, a long-necked flexible flashlight that can be used for illuminating hard-to-reach corners or behind-the-scenes angles. The SnakeLight Dual Beam doubles as a flashlight and a lamp capable of lighting up a wide area.

Had the company relied only on its product development team, however, the SnakeLight might never have wound around the corners of consumers' minds. Black & Decker actually created three prototypes of new flashlights, including the SnakeLight, which was never the favorite of company managers. When they offered consumers the three choices for their comments, managers were surprised to discover that consumers preferred the SnakeLight.

According to Mike Brennan, vice president of engineering for consumer products, "Sometimes we at the company are too close to the products, and we fail to see what value they may have for end users. Sometimes we really like a product that our consumers don't like. We're always ready to listen to them, however, and in the case of the SnakeLight, I'm glad we did."

But Black & Decker does more than just listen to its consumers. It directly *involves* them in the creation and refinement of products, and the results are outstanding. The company's VersaPak line of cordless power tools brought in some $100 million in 1997, and the number of tools in the lineup has steadily increased—from three in 1994, 25 in 1996, and 50 or more in 1998. The story behind the development of the VersaPak line offers several insights into the process of involving customers in the design of products and services.

In 1988, Black & Decker made a prototype of a new battery-powered cordless screwdriver that it hoped to sell to professionals and serious do-it-yourselfers. Unlike earlier models, this prototype would allow consumers to remove the battery from the handle and use it in another Black & Decker cordless product. After initial research indicated that there was no market for such a tool, the company shelved the product for four years.

Then, in 1992, Skil Corporation came out with its own tool system called Flexicharge, which offered consumers interchangeable batteries. The cordless tool market had undergone a number of changes in that four-year period, as Black & Decker learned through customer interviews and surveys. People had begun to understand the value of removable and rechargeable batteries, a lesson they learned from using camcorders, cordless and cellular telephones, and other such products. Consumers also complained that earlier versions of cordless tools became useless when the batteries went bad, and they ended up throwing the entire product away rather than replacing its batteries.

Black & Decker sent company representatives to numerous Kmarts, Home Depots, and Wal-Marts to survey potential consumers about what they wanted in a battery-powered cordless tool. Recognizing that it already had the technology, the company dusted off its 1988 prototype, refined the product according to the information gathered in the store surveys, and in 1994 produced its VersaPak line of tools for do-it-yourselfers.

At first the VersaPak line included only a drill, a screwdriver, and a flashlight. The company has added more than 30 products since then and has plans for perhaps another 20, including sanders, blade trimmers, grass shears, and cordless brooms. The great advantage of the VersaPak system is that the same batteries, easily removed and recharged, work in all the products. And this convenience has made for a very profitable product.

According to Brennan, the key to such success lies in the company's ability to talk directly to its end users. "Black & Decker," he says, "is world-class at getting the voice of the consumer." The company does not merely send a marketing team out to talk to consumers, it sends out an entire company team—manufacturers, engineers, marketers, salespeople, and customer service representatives. Sometimes this group parks a VersaPak van outside a Wal-Mart, floats a big VersaPak balloon above the parking lot, and invites customers to test the product on shrubs, lumber, or whatever might be found in a home repair shop. In addition, the Black & Decker team trains salespeople at various stores to instruct consumers in the use of VersaPak.

Whether your company makes pizzas or peat moss, swimming pools or pool tables, the lessons of Black & Decker are invaluable: At their peril, companies exclude customers from the design and creation of products and services. Fierce competition today forces companies to become much more flexible and creative in their dealings with customers to give them *exactly* what they want.

Once a company thoroughly understands its customers' wants and needs and effectively segments markets to capture value, it can begin the second main process: *involving customers in the design of products and services*. For many managers and employees this process requires a rethinking of fundamental assumptions about the relationship between a company and its customers. Like Black & Decker, successful companies are continually looking for ways to implement the three main subprocesses necessary to this process:

- Develop new concepts and plans for products and services.
- Design, build, and evaluate prototypes and pilot services.

- Refine and customize products or services, then test their effectiveness.

As we saw in chapter 3, a myriad of ways to involve customers makes this process economically and logistically possible: A company can mail out surveys, conduct telephone interviews, put up Internet bulletin boards, write follow-up letters, open customer service centers, provide toll-free customer response numbers, and establish customer advisory panels and focus groups. Consumers' responses will quickly point out where and why a company's products and services fail to satisfy, but for the most part these reasons fall into a single category: They do not meet customers' needs and wants.

While there is no simple formula for developing successful products, more and more companies are looking to their customers to tell them exactly what they want. That way, they reduce the need for future revisions and, even better, enhance the chances of the product's success. They look for ways to solidify the relationship with the customer and build customer loyalty. In addition, they set priorities for product design and development, making better use of resources, according to their customers' needs. This is what Black & Decker did in developing its Snake-Light and VersaPak line of cordless power tools, and as we will see, similar processes have had extraordinary results at best-practice companies such as Varian Associates, GE Plastics, and The Walt Disney Company.

By gathering information from customers at each stage of product development, designers and manufacturers can "tweak" the product to make it fit customers' expectations, even as these change during the course of development. An advertising executive may design multiple campaigns to show a client, who then has a chance to offer input on designs and participate in the final decision. AMP, supplier of electrical circuits and connectors, has perfected the subprocess of collaborating directly with its customers in the design and refinement of products. Its best practice lies primarily in product customization.

Incorporating all three subprocesses, the best-practice company and its customers can begin to think of the company-client relationship as a *partnership* rather than two "ships" passing in the night. The term *partnership* we take not so much in its legal definition of co-ownership but rather in its sense of sharing in profits and losses of the company. If a customer partners with Dell Computer in the design of his or her personal computer, and Dell can thereby direct more efficiently the use of its resources, both customer and company profit. Dell Computer makes and sells only what the customer needs, and the customer reaps the benefits by getting that customized product at a quality price.

In this chapter, we present several examples of best-practice companies that have implemented these processes to improve the products and services they deliver.

Subprocess 1
Develop New Concepts and Plans for
Products and Services

While many companies conduct surveys of their customers to gauge their satisfaction, not all that many systematically take advantage of the information they gather or bring customers together in focus groups to exchange ideas about what they seek in a product. The first step in developing new concepts and plans for products and services is to listen to your customers and take seriously what they tell you. This includes having the foresight to uncover those *latent* needs that customers may not verbally express but, once implemented, will undoubtedly please them. As products like the Sony Walkman have proven, giving people what they don't yet know they want can be a very profitable (even if risky) practice.

Second, set up as many lines of communication as possible, both within the company and between company representatives and customers. Not only salespeople should talk to service representatives and executive officers, but all should share information with the customer regarding new products and services. They can solicit feedback at every stage: What do customers want and need?

SOLECTRON

Recognizing its success in involving customers in the production of products and services, the magazine *Enjeux-Les Echos* and Arthur Andersen awarded the 1997 Client Satisfaction prize to electronics manufacturer Solectron. In France, Solectron's achievement signals a major national shift in attitude toward treating customers with respect.

To remind employees how *not* to treat customers, Solectron hung posters in its corridors depicting caricatures of the worst customer service representatives. According to *Enjeux-Les Echos* (April 1997), Solectron distinguished itself among French companies for its excellence in involving customers in products and services. In this regard, the caricatures are no laughing matter.

On one wall is Raymond Jargon, master of euphemisms as tangled as the webs of misinformation he spins to placate dissatisfied customers. On another wall appears Rita Sarcasm, whose biting wit can wither any inquiring customer. And down another corridor hangs a picture of Rosemonde None-of-My-Business, that paragon of the "not invented here" response to customer service.

But Solectron goes further than merely satirizing the Worst

Employees of the Year. The company opens its doors to its most valued customers. Each of thirty primary clients has a specially designated space inside the Solectron plant in Bordeaux where customer representatives collaborate with Solectron engineers to design and build electronic parts. According to Jean-Marie Reilhac, director of quality at Solectron, some of the company's largest clients, such as Hewlett-Packard, are so intimately integrated into product design and manufacturing that Solectron employees even wear the client's logo on their uniforms.

This symbiotic relationship also takes place at the customer's site. A Solectron engineer, for instance, works full-time at 3Com's Israel facility, which builds informational electronic networks. Moreover, as Reilhac points out, Solectron enjoys a direct line of communication with HP Ecosse, a major customer, providing firsthand knowledge of inventories and thereby giving Solectron a competitive advantage over other subcontractors.

VARIAN ASSOCIATES, INC.

Headquartered in Palo Alto, California, Varian Associates, Inc., produces sophisticated health care systems, semiconductor manufacturing equipment, and instruments used in pharmaceuticals, chemicals, petroleum, and other industries. With manufacturing facilities in nine nations—Australia, Finland, France, Great Britain, Italy, Japan, Korea, Switzerland, and the United States—Varian recently won distinction for the third straight year as the top company in customer satisfaction, according to the prestigious VLSI Research, Inc., survey. Given that its customers are extremely demanding, the distinctive ranking has inspired many other companies to benchmark against Varian.

Varian's customers form an elite group. For the health care industry, the company manufactures radiation therapy systems such as Clinac, which is used in treating cancerous tumors, and software programs such as VARIS, a network that integrates all aspects of cancer therapy. For analytical researchers and laboratories, Varian produces its UltraMass ICP-MS system, which can detect minute quantities of contaminants in drinking water or the environment. And between 1995 and 1997 the company revised its entire line of nuclear magnetic resonance spectrometers to make them easier to use and more sensitive instruments for analytical research.

According to Allen Lauer, executive vice president, Varian owes much of its success to customers who participate directly in the creation of these innovative products. "Our customers tell us what their problems are, but they can't always see an immediate solution to them. Since a new product takes at least two or three years to develop, by that time the specifications have changed, and the product may no longer suit the customer's needs. That's why we try to extrapolate as far into the future as we can."

As Lauer explains, a team of Varian researchers, marketers, and technical experts meets with customers to identify specific problems and set priorities on needs. Varian's Ginzton Research Center in Palo Alto often provides the setting where ideas find their way to the drawing board, as engineers come up with a solution and build a prototype. In the early 1990s, for instance, Varian worked with customers such as the Hazardous Waste Research and Information Center at the University of Illinois at Urbana-Champaign to develop an ICP-MS (inductively coupled plasma mass spectrometer) system that can analyze samples with speed and accuracy. Focus groups also gave Varian researchers valuable information about features to be excluded; for instance, they suggested that the new system did not need the capacity to test for negative ions but did need to provide modem connection for diagnosing samples at remote locations. The collaboration of Varian researchers and customers resulted in the innovative UltraMass ICP-MS, which can detect metals at parts-per-trillion levels—the equivalent of looking for a single human hair on a railway track that wraps twice around the equator!

Varian has learned the tremendous value that customers can bring to product development, and it actively seeks that input whenever possible. One such innovation recently came from several thousand miles away.

In Walnut Creek, California, Varian's Chromatography Systems Business manufactures instruments known as gas chromatographs, which chemists use to separate and measure volatile substances such as gasoline and semivolatile substances, including drugs and pesticides. Using a new technology called SPME (solid phase micro extraction), researchers can extract those chemicals from samples in water and analyze them with a gas chromatograph. Varian has automated this technology, making it a relatively quick method for concentrating very small quantities of impurities in a sample.

SPME worked well for volatile chemicals, but molecules with higher boiling points required mixing to be extracted from water. Because the automated system was not designed to mix samples, a redesign was required.

The solution came from almost eight thousand miles away. Dr. Helmut Geppert of Lausitzer Wasser GmbH, a Varian customer in Germany, devised an ingenious plan that he shared with Wulf Koehler, a Varian engineer. Together they rigged up a motor from an electric shaver and attached it to the coated fiber suspended in the aqueous solution. The gentle vibrations stirred the waters just enough to release the semivolatile substances more quickly.

Further refinements of the invention led to a joint patent held by Dr. Geppert and Varian, which has incorporated the technology into its new SPME III autosampler. Not only has the innovation won praises from other customers, but it has also opened up an entirely new sector of the market for Varian Chromatography Systems.

In part as a result of this productive collaboration between company and customer, Varian has permanently established a customer advisory board to assess customers' feelings on product concepts. Supporting the company's ongoing research and development of new and refined products, the board has been instrumental in creating an atmosphere at Varian where focus groups have a real say in the creative effort.

In some cases, a company may find it equally valuable to send its representatives to a customer's facility. Providing on-site observation and expertise to help clients learn how to best use the product or service becomes yet another means of building a best practice. This is more, however, than just sending out one of your salespeople or technical service representatives to plug in a computer or glad-hand a company CEO. It means installing full-time employees at your expense in the factories, warehouses, and even the boardrooms of companies you do business with. The lines of communication extended to your customer should be free of middlemen: No one should need to leave a message on voice mail. Your clients receive immediate feedback rather than waiting days or weeks for a response. Meanwhile, your representatives can attend the client's design and engineering meetings as well as participate in plans to advertise, market, and distribute a product or service. In short, this process creates an instantaneous and highly profitable exchange of information between groups that would otherwise meet sporadically if at all.

GE PLASTICS

For the employees of GE Plastics of Pittsfield, Massachusetts, *kaizen* is more than a popular term borrowed from Japanese management to refer to "continuous improvement." It's a way of life and a way of doing business. Taking its cue from the automobile industry, where the concept gained a stronghold in the last two decades, GE Plastics has introduced the philosophy to its customers. In fact, over 165 GE Plastics customers are now involved with GE using this approach, and the company saved them over $120 million in 1996 alone.

A subsidiary of General Electric, GE Plastics does much more than develop new applications for polymers and resins. It does that, too, of course; for example, the company helped design the "Super Plug," an automobile door module that combines over 60 parts and components into a single piece. But GE Plastics is equally well known for working closely with customers to help them solve problems and improve productivity.

"We don't want to do things *to* our customers to save money," says Sandy Torony, general manager of customer productivity programs at GE Plastics. "We want to do it *with* them."

To accomplish this goal, commercial field and technical personnel from GE Plastics go into a customer's organization by invitation to study production processes, assess problems, and identify opportunities for taking cost out of operations. "We often act as a new pair of eyes," says Torony, "seeing a process from an angle that the customer may never have considered. We also have experts within our business that our customers would ordinarily not have access to." The GEP team may spend three or four days "in shop," up to 24 hours a day, in order to measure cycle time and determine ways to improve the customer's production. Although the scrutiny of the initial few days can be intense, the typical assessment program runs four or five months, with occasional visits to monitor progress and make adjustments in production.

Sometimes the solution is a relatively simple one, such as bringing in an expert from another GE component, perhaps GE

Lighting. One customer, for example, had difficulty identifying scrap materials in one part of its plant, sometimes throwing out the good with the bad, but the GE Plastics team solved the problem and vastly improved performance by flipping the idea switch that illuminated the customer's manufacturing plant through new lighting systems.

By working directly with its customers—indeed, by working in their own shops—GE Plastics can come to a deeper understanding of its customers as well as their relationship with suppliers, of whom it is one. In 1996, the company saved its compact disc customers over $10 million by improving the plastic used in CDs to meet customers' specifications.

According to Bob Hess, manager of communications at GE Plastics, this direct participation has given the company a huge competitive advantage. "Customers have asked us to help them deal with complex business problems such as health care costs, employee compensation analysis, and time-to-market product development. To fill this need, GE Plastics has to understand markets and customers thoroughly."

JIT II: BOSE AND ITS SUPPLIERS

In 1987, Lance Dixon, director of purchasing and logistics at the Bose Corporation, a manufacturer of high-fidelity audio systems, came up with a startling idea. Why not "remove" the salesperson, buyer, and planner from the typical relationship Bose had with its suppliers? The result of this question was the creation of JIT II, a refinement of the just-in-time inventory system. But rather than handling inventory, JIT II creates a new relationship between Bose and its customer, a relationship that has now been implemented nationally in hundreds of companies, including Honeywell, IBM, and Westinghouse.

In this model the supplier, at his or her own expense, "in-plants" one or more full-time employees at its customer's site. Those workers have full authority to conduct transactions between supplier and customer, attend the meetings of engineering and design teams to help refine products or services, gather crucial marketing and sales information, and gauge the customer's present and future needs. Equipped with this information, these in-plants report back to the supplier in real time so that production and inventory can be adjusted as quickly and cost-effectively as possible.

This symbiotic relationship not only saves valuable time at the supplier end but also lowers overhead costs for the customer who enjoys several added benefits. Assuming the role of "customer," the Bose Corporation, for example, creates a space for representatives of its various suppliers who provide welcomed expertise in the creation of audio equipment. At the same time, Bose employees profit from the stimulus of imaginative suggestions for improved design and engineering of its products.

According to Lance Dixon, "You no longer have information being handed off from a material planner to a buyer, who then hands it off to a salesman, who eventually hands it off back to his plant. Three or four of those transactions are now occurring within the mind of one individual with the authority to act. It's seamless."

Moreover, the JIT II system radically alters the transportation modes that have traditionally defined the connections between supplier and customer when applied to a company's logistics functions. Whether supplies come by land, sea, or air, whether they cross state or international boundaries, one group of in-plants from Roadway Trucking, ocean freight lines, and the Tower division of McGraw-Hill (an import/export customs broker) can sit in the Bose command center and direct the traffic each step of the way. Dixon says the company "plays that supply chain like an orchestra. The process has taken the coordination of three multiple-billion-dollar organizations down to three guys named Bob, Ralph, and Harry, who stand up over cubicles and say, 'I've got the Bose ocean shipment coming in to Seattle in three days. You get your plane in there, and I've got the truck lined up to meet it!'"

The examples of GE Plastics, Varian Associates, and Bose Corporation provide ample evidence that collaborating with customers in the creation and refinement of products and services leads to strong, profitable "partnerships." Allowing customers to be part of your decision-making process—in effect, making the customers your partners—creates a sense of co-ownership of those products and services. A customer who special-orders a Dell computer assumes the role of creative partner with the company as it customizes that product. The customer will most likely remain loyal to Dell as long as the company continues to flourish and develop even better products.

Subprocess 2
Design, Build, and Evaluate Prototypes

Concerned by declining market share in the mid-1980s that suggested consumers were growing to prefer the sweeter taste of Pepsi to Coke, the Coca-Cola Company did what seemed rational for a number one company losing ground to number two: It test-marketed a sweetened version of its own ninety-nine-year-old formula. When nearly 200,000 blind taste tests confirmed that the new formula was preferred to the old, the company released its "New Coke" to the public in 1985—and discontinued the original version.

Assuming that customers would enjoy this switch, Coca-Cola

launched a huge advertising campaign to promote the new taste. As is widely known, the results were disastrous. The company underestimated the power of the Coke brand, despite what the drink tasted like. (In the few tests where tasters *did* know which formula was which, the original formula usually won out.) Three months of vocal consumer dissatisfaction prompted the company to re-release the old formula under the name "Classic Coke," and subsequent ads focused increasingly on the unwavering dependability that customers demanded: "Always Coca-Cola." As chairman Roberto Goizueta would later tell *Fortune* magazine, "New Coke made us realize Coca-Cola was more than a flavor or a bottle. It was a mental attitude." This lesson cost Goizueta's company $35 million.

Savvy companies learn from such incidents and take steps to embrace their customers' ideas and loyalty in every way possible. In designing a new product, these companies involve customers by capturing their total input, conducting feasibility studies, and actually building the prototype. They don't blindly test a new product against an old one; they find out exactly how customers feel about *both*—in their hearts as much as their taste buds—then make decisions accordingly.

AMP, Inc.

With operating centers in Europe, Asia, and the Americas, AMP is widely known as a manufacturer of electrical and electronic connectors. It produces more than 100,000 terminals, assemblies, and other components supplied to thousands of OEM customers worldwide, customers as large as IBM, General Electric, Boeing, Toyota, and Daimler-Benz.

AMP has implemented a rapid-prototype development program through which it assesses the needs of its customers and those of *their* customers. Part of the company's success can be attributed to its concurrent engineering team, which can design and redesign a product while it is being critiqued by customers, even before the prototype is built. This close involvement with customers allows AMP to bring a product from the drawing board to the shelf in under twelve weeks, a series of steps that in the past could have taken a year or more.

Using rapid prototyping, the company actually puts together a team of designers, manufacturers, engineers, and safety experts, who build, test, and improve on products by presenting them in digital format to customers. Computer-aided design, or CAD, programs enable a manufacturer to create a model that customers can "use" before it goes to the expense of building and producing it. In this way, the AMP team works with its customers to discover where the problems with the design occur, and it can correct them, usually within a very short time.

When a defense contractor, for example, needed an interconnect board for use in a supercomputer, AMP employees teamed up with in-house engineers to create a prototype and test and analyze the system—a year faster than the contractor could have done it alone. Using quality functional deployment, or QFD, the company builds products to order, setting priorities according to the customer's specifications. At present, QFD is used chiefly in the automotive industry, as illustrated by the connectors that AMP designs and tests for Lexus. According to Dean Hooper, vice president of global customer satisfaction and business effectiveness at AMP, "We make sure that our development and engineering people meet face-to-face with customers in order to learn what those customers need and how they can make the best use of our products. Through computer-aided engineering (CAE) and directly linked numerical control (NC) equipment, we can produce a plastic mockup of a product in a matter of hours rather than months, thus giving customers something they can hold in their hands."

Taking this process one step beyond computer-aided design, AMP recently built an Internet site *(www.connectamp.com)* that presents its entire catalog of products. A customer can call up the Web page, locate a product or a part that fits the specifications of a particular project, and download a three-dimensional design directly into an application to determine whether it will fit properly. Operating on a worldwide basis, the site communicates in eight languages to 98,000 registered users in nearly 140 countries. On a typical day, AMP's Internet site receives more than 90,000 "hits."

As a best-practice enterprise, AMP demonstrates how a company can build an enormous range of products—in this case more than 100,000 of them—and give its customers the added benefits of production speed, precision, and interactivity in finding the item that fits their needs precisely. In designing and testing products with its customers, AMP sets the standard for doing it fast and doing it right the first time. The company has learned that it cannot wait six months to begin prototyping since by that time the customer's needs might change and the product will no longer be needed.

Subprocess 3
Refine and Customize Products or Services, Then Test Their Effectiveness

Ask them and they will come. Long left out of the developmental stages of products and services, customers now take a much more active role in the creation of their own personal computers, perfect-fit blue jeans, even made-to-order automobiles. True, customization is much easier in some industries than in others: The strategy of one-size-fits-all works well if your company makes socks or ponchos, but other enterprises are hoping to capture the attention of today's discriminating customers who want to be a part of the process of creating the products they need.

By inviting customers to join you in this process, you can take the first steps toward the ideal state of "made to order." Usually this ideal implies a single individual: Each customer receives blue jeans tailor-made or an accounting service specially designed for the corner restaurant. But many companies begin with a broader definition of "customization." They start with one of their existing products or services—which may have served a segment of the market well for years but for which sales have slipped—and ask their customers what kinds of improvements they would make to it.

Refining an existing product or service doesn't mean simply changing those already in your arsenal. Those items may indeed belong to your closest competitor, or they may once have failed to capture the public's attention and now gather dust on your warehouse shelves. After all, what's wrong with improving on what someone else has done—even if that someone else is yourself? This is exactly what Black & Decker did in developing and marketing its VersaPak system of tools for the home and garden.

The trick comes in *refining* the product or service. Merely repackaging it won't do. In some cases, you can make changes in how it is marketed or delivered—as FedEx has demonstrated with its online package ordering and tracking options—but to complete such a first-rate refinement, take your customers' ideas to heart and to the design board.

THE WALT DISNEY COMPANY

Refinements in products and services at the Disney theme parks have made many of its more than 70 million annual visitors applaud. Among the hundreds of thousands of letters the company received in one recent year were several from writers complaining that their children had had few opportunities to meet the Disney characters and to have their pictures taken with Mickey Mouse. Here was clearly an area needing improvement, and as Disney officials saw it, what better opportunity to refine an existing service than dressing employees up like Mickey Mouse and other characters to roam the park and greet customers?

First, the company created a new facility called Mickey's Starland. Here Mickey has a dressing room where kids can enter, sit in his lap, and have a personal picture taken. Next, Disney planners established "character breakfasts" throughout the resort to guarantee that guests could actually meet the likes of Jiminy Cricket or the Seven Dwarfs. In short, the company improved an existing service—the visibility and access to characters, especially Mickey—by setting aside areas designed for a particular segment of visitors, namely parents with young children. The refined services directly involve those specific customers who requested them, but with added benefits for all visitors: More Mickeys make everyone happy.

BEST-PRACTICE AGENDA

Survey customers for their opinions, ideas, feelings, likes, and dislikes about products or services. Whenever possible, meet them face-to-face to discuss their views. Most important, listen closely to what they have to say.

From these surveys and other customer interactions, collect, categorize, and deliver information about product use to the people in your organization who need it.

Describe to your customers how they can help you understand their needs, then create products and services that meet those demands. Define the values that this step of the process has for them: more precisely customized products and services, speedier development, increased opportunities to participate in the design stages, and greater savings in production and use.

Make refinements in existing products and services, partnering with your customers either on their premises or yours when possible. Share information both at home and at the customer's site.

Test the refinement in a controlled environment with targeted segments of customers.

Market the successfully refined product, but keep the doors open to further improvements as you receive suggestions from your customers and as their needs change.

Top Ten Best-Practice Diagnostic Questions

1. How do you gather customer input about product design and use? Telephone or mail surveys? Internet bulletin boards? Focus groups? Feasibility studies?

2. Do you have a team comprising representatives from various groups—manufacturing, engineering, marketing, sales, and so forth—that goes out to meet with customers?

3. Have you ever allowed your customers to decide whether or not you should implement a change, as Disney did in creating Mickey's Starland and character breakfasts?

4. To what extent do you involve customers in the design of prototypes? What about *their* customers?

5. Do you look for customer insights before making refinements or customization changes to existing products, as Black & Decker did in creating its VersaPak line?

6. Do you get wisdom and insights from customers at each step of development? Do you have a customer advisory board?

7. Do you partner with customers so that they allow your em

ployees to visit their sites? If so, how many of these relationships do you have?

8. Do you have space reserved in your plant for *your* best clients (or suppliers) to collaborate with you in design, production, and other areas? (A mailbox slot or coffee mug doesn't count.)

9. How much do you share information with clients? Do you give them the right to attend design and engineering meetings? Get input on upcoming advertising and sales campaigns?

10. How easy is it for clients to reach someone at your company with a proposed change or refinement? How long does it take your company to respond? How many people get to see and discuss the proposal?

CHAPTER 5

FACE-TO-FACE AND EAR-TO-EAR

How to Market and Sell Products and Services

SUBPROCESSES

SECURE CHANNELS OF DISTRIBUTION
ESTABLISH PRICING
DEVELOP ADVERTISING AND PROMOTION STRATEGIES
DEVELOP AND DEPLOY A SALES FORCE
PROCESS ORDERS
DEVELOP CUSTOMERS

BEST-PRACTICE COMPANIES

LEXUS DIVISION OF TOYOTA MOTORS
DELL COMPUTER
PEAPOD
SOUTHWEST AIRLINES
NIKE
CUTLER-HAMMER
ALLEGIANCE HEALTHCARE

AMERICAN AIRLINES
ENRON

n 1989—without a secure base of loyal customers, without an immediately recognizable brand name, without a track record for service and quality, and without a sales force trained in the new product—the Lexus division of Toyota Motor Corporation set its sights on capturing a major share of the U.S. luxury car market. Such barriers to entry would have frightened off most newcomers, but as we noted in chapter 3, Lexus drew confidence from the vast and efficient system of Toyota suppliers at its disposal. Still, there were risks. Luxury car customers were a much smaller segment of the overall market than its parent company Toyota was used to dealing with. Although prospering and apparently steady, the U.S. economy showed signs of cracks and fissures. And the gleaming likes of Cadillac, Lincoln, Mercedes-Benz, BMW, and newcomer Infiniti seemed formidable opponents.

Undaunted, Lexus moved quickly, taking advantage of the production capability established by Toyota and creating its own channels of distribution. The company initially set target prices at $40,000 for its cars, significantly lower than comparable Mercedes-Benz models and other luxury lines. It blitzed the market with advertising to build an image of its cars as fresh, sleek alternatives to lumbering Cadillacs and Lincolns and harsh-riding Mercedes and BMW products.

With a clear strategic plan to establish the best trained and most responsive sales force, Lexus studied best-practice companies such as retail giant Nordstrom, a company known for setting high standards for itself and its salespeople. The auto company then began negotiating with upscale dealers who could offer an atmosphere of quality and prestige attractive to new customers. Moreover, it recognized that many of those potential customers wanted to lease vehicles (today, in fact, almost two-thirds of Lexus customers lease their cars).

The company still thoroughly trains its salespeople and service technicians in the intricacies of each new model. No matter how long they have been with the company, Lexus *retrains* them every year, and all associates must pass a test certifying them on product knowledge and customer service skills. The company emphasizes the need to build a personal relationship with each customer from the initial contact through the purchase or lease and into the "ownership experience." From the start, Lexus dealers distinguished themselves for great personal service, and many of them even visit customers' homes to deliver new cars or resolve complaints. The company rewards its best dealers by tying compensation to customer satisfaction, not to revenues.

Lexus installed a completely integrated computer system that allows a dealer anywhere in the United States to find a car at another dealership or in transit from its hub in Long Beach, California, and have it shipped to a customer in Orlando or Minneapolis within days. Its system for processing orders has proven to be extremely efficient in meeting customers' expectations. Lexus understands that its customers want to be treated well in

what is traditionally a stressful transaction. "We treat our customers as though they're coming to our home—with respect and dignity," says Steven Sturm, corporate marketing manager at Lexus. "We treat them like that from the time they buy a car all the way until they're ready to trade it in and buy a new one. Treat them right the first time, and they'll come back and be loyal to you."

Over 500,000 loyal customers serve as evidence that Lexus has established itself as a best-practice company in the six subprocesses associated with marketing and selling products: (1) Secure channels of distribution, (2) establish pricing, (3) develop advertising and promotion strategies, (4) develop and deploy a sales force, (5) process orders, and (6) develop customers. By mastering these subprocesses, Lexus captured 30 of a possible 40 major awards from J. D. Power and Associates from 1989 to 1997, more than any other automobile company during that period.

Subprocess 1
Secure Channels of Distribution

The search to find more efficient and less costly ways to reach existing or new customers continues to inspire—but at times perplex—the best minds in business. Traditionally, most companies have had a very limited channel of distribution. Either they employed a sales force that met with customers one at a time, or they contracted with a few distributors, or they worked with a limited number of retailers to get products to market.

Years of restructuring have led many companies to look more critically at those traditional channels of distribution. By investigating multiple channels, they hope to expand into new markets and secure a sales base. In the early 1980s, for example, when the computer industry began directing sales toward individual consumers, its channel of distribution was relatively narrow because it was directed primarily toward large businesses. Later, as marketers promoted the products and as the public began to recognize the need for personal computers, many new channels opened up, from the corner discount house to retailers in shopping malls to direct catalog sales.

Aggressive, forward-thinking companies now use a systematic approach to uncover or create innovative channels of distribution.

Those companies can either work in a typical manufacturer-distributor-retailer chain or pool their resources with other producers to gain exposure to one another's markets. Best-practice companies frequently seek to broaden these distribution channels by engaging in direct selling, telemarketing, direct mail, or Internet efforts.

DELL COMPUTER CORPORATION

The phenomenal success of Dell Computer Corporation rests squarely on its innovative and finely tuned distribution channel of direct sales to customers. In fiscal year 1997, sales grew 47 percent, more than twice as much as the overall computer industry grew.

Fortune 500 companies, two-person businesses, government agencies, health care and educational institutions, as well as individuals have direct access to the computer manufacturer through various toll-free telephone numbers, over the Internet *(www.dell.com)*, and face-to-face in the case of large corporate and institutional accounts. Customers can receive product information, place orders, or speak directly to a Dell representative who can fax back a quotation within minutes.

Far less expensive than traditional channels, which use resellers and middlemen, the direct approach, according to founder Michael Dell, "eliminates reseller markup and speeds up the flow of inventory." Under this system, the company can turn around a customer's order in five days, typically at a cost 10 percent to 20 percent lower than the customer would pay at a retail outlet. It also allows the company to move new technology such as advanced Pentium chips into its product lines faster.

How does Dell Computer achieve such profitable efficiency? It has become the master of the vertical distribution channel by serving as the sole distributor of its products and services. There are typically six steps in that process:

1. A customer initiates the process by contacting the company via telephone or the Internet. A customer can order from Dell online 24 hours a day or by phone from early morning until late in the evening. As Michael Dell puts it, "We have three ways of selling: We do it face-to-face; we do it ear-to-ear; and we do it keyboard-to-server."

2. A Dell representative can make suggestions and help customers determine what systems will best meet their needs. Through the Web site, customers can access product information and receive price estimates instantaneously. During the first quarter of 1997, the company sold $1 million worth of products *daily* on its Internet site.

3. A Dell representative confirms the order and verifies the financial credit charge. Usually, the representative promises that the computer will arrive within five business days, although the customer often receives the product quicker than this.

4. The Dell factory receives a printout of the order and begins manufacturing within hours. Each computer is custom-built and put through several hardware and software tests in less than one day.

5. After a final inspection, the computer is boxed by Dell and sent to a distribution center that ships it by a carrier in time to arrive with a monitor that is built ahead of time by a separate supplier.

6. From this point on, customers have direct access to the company's extensive service support network, 24 hours a day. The company also offers next-day onsite service for up to five years, depending on the type of warranty a customer orders.

As Michael Dell puts it, "Ours is an execution-based, model-driven business. We've never had any finished inventory, nor do we want any." One way Dell Computer beats its competitors on prices is by keeping component inventories to a minimum. Vertical integration has helped the company further reduce costs. Monitors, for example, are relatively standardized and built by a supplier. As Dell says, "Today I need 8,742 monitors; tomorrow I might need 962. One of our carriers simply picks them up at night while we're all sleeping, matches them up with the PCs by purchase order, and the next day delivers them to the customers."

Vertical integration and direct marketing are the keys to Dell Computer's vibrant success. The company has locked up the distribution channel by clearly identifying its markets and by designing products and services to fit the needs of its customers. According to Michael Dell, "The direct contact with our customers gives us minute-by-minute input—from the largest customer to the individual—in terms of what products they like and what new services they'd like to see us develop."

PEAPOD, INC.

Having opened in 1989 in Evanston, Illinois, Peapod, Inc., the online grocery store, now has over 51,000 members in eight metropolitan areas, including Chicago, San Francisco–San Jose, Columbus, Houston, Dallas, Austin, Atlanta, and Boston. With plans to expand that market to more than 100,000 in the near future, the company determined that all a customer needed was a computer and a modem to make one-stop shopping on the Internet a reality and give the company a share of the $400 billion grocery industry in the next decade.

Peapod has secured its channels of distribution by installing a 60 gigabyte Informix database running on a Hewlett-Packard HP9000 server. That technology allows the company to accomplish several goals essential to controlling its distribution chain. It can track every purchase customers make and thus create customer profiles to use when promoting special offers and advertisements. "If you buy diapers," says CEO and founder Andrew Parkinson, "we know you have a kid. If you buy dog food, we know you have a dog." Most other competitors have been unable to match this degree of data collection about their target markets. The HP9000 server, for example, knows every item a customer has purchased for three consecutive orders. When that customer signs onto Peapod's Internet site, a "grocery list" of those favorite items, unique to each customer, is waiting on screen.

The database also enables Peapod to keep close tabs on inventory with its partners, the large grocery chains located in major markets—Jewel Osco in Chicago, Safeway in San Francisco, Stop & Shop in Boston, for example. At present the company is located inside the various grocery stores themselves, operating as a distributor for the large chains. "We don't pay rent," says Parkinson, "we're partners with the retailers. They outsource to us everything that we can do more cheaply than they can do themselves. We manage the online service, the member support, the picking, the packing, and the delivery."

This service gives Peapod a direct link into customers' homes and creates one-to-one marketing that retail grocery chains can neither afford nor develop effectively on their own. Peapod, according to Parkinson, "provides the expertise in the distribution channel." If a Peapod "ambassador" breaks a dozen eggs while delivering an order, the customer has an immediate contact point to issue a complaint and get satisfaction.

The Peapod database has proved so successful that the company can now sell its information, thereby securing additional channels of distribution. "We are selling licenses to Peapod systems across industries and to international organizations," says

Parkinson. It does so by eliminating the expensive bricks and mortar of real estate that grocery stores have to maintain, not to mention the high cost of inventories.

Peapod has made a best practice of not only dealing with channels of distribution that already exist (manufacturer to distributor to end user), but also establishing and securing new channels by training customers to shop through this online service.

Subprocess 2
Establish Pricing

Many say that price is the single most important communicator of what a company wants to say about a product or service. As Lexus illustrates in establishing its prices for luxury cars, a company can use pricing strategy to solidify its market position and build perceptions of value and quality in the minds of its customers.

An optimal pricing strategy touches just the right nerve. Such a strategy should balance customer demand with a company's internal financial constraints. Managers should find the point at which the company can maximize its profits while still giving customers the high value they seek. The shrewdest of managers know profitability is built by capturing more value, not necessarily by making more sales. In short, the product value—its strengths and weaknesses, its competitive positioning, and its distribution power—drives the pricing strategy.

The company's next step in this subprocess is monitoring its own price performance as well as that of its competitors. This is essential both in determining past market behavior and in projecting future trends. Companies such as Lexus and Southwest Airlines deliberately set prices lower than competitors' in order to build up their customer base. As a secondary result, their pricing strategies lead the competition to lower its prices as well.

When the competition heats up, as it has done in the luxury car market and in the airline industry, companies continually adjust their market strategies and look for ways to reduce their costs in order to relieve pricing pressures. They frequently pass these savings on to their best customers through lower prices and greater improvements in product quality.

SOUTHWEST AIRLINES

"No frills flying" at Southwest Airlines came about when the company initially established its pricing *not* according to what competitor airlines were charging but, rather, on the prices that bus companies and rental car agencies had set for trips of comparable distance. Today, as Kathy Pettit, director for customers, explains, when passengers board a Southwest plane, they know exactly what they are getting: "A good, clean, safe, on-time, efficient product, delivered with a smile." Instead of lunch, passengers receive a bag of peanuts humorously labeled "frills."

Even chairman and president Herb Kelleher appears on the cover of Kevin and Jackie Freiberg's *Nuts: Southwest Airlines' Crazy Recipe for Business and Personal Success* sporting a tattoo on his right arm that reads "Still Nuts After All These Years." Whether it's a description of lunch or a synonym for a wild and wacky way of doing business, *nuts* epitomizes Southwest's philosophy and practice. And nothing in the company dramatizes that philosophy and practice better than its pricing policy.

Southwest has never concealed the fact that it views the automobile and the highway as its main competition. "It's not American Airlines," says Pettit, speaking of the company's strategies in setting such low fares. Although the company keeps a close eye on what the other airlines are doing, it looks outside its industry at other modes of transportation to determine its pricing policies.

In a business where pricing can fluctuate wildly, Southwest maintains its competitive edge by knowing exactly what people are willing to pay for a ticket. "If the fare is $79," says Pettit, "you have a certain percentage of people who won't go, no matter what. If the fare is $59, you still find a number of people who won't go. As fares go lower and lower, the birds start buying the tickets."

Five months after the airline began operations in 1971, Southwest offered a seat on a Friday night flight from Houston to Dallas for only $10. Later, when Braniff priced its tickets for the same route at $81, Texas International came in at $56, but Southwest continued to undercut them both by offering a fare of a mere $24. Today, the ticket costs around $70, but that is still cheaper than any other airline can offer on an unrestricted basis. How does Southwest consistently come up with the lowest fares to offer its customers? The management team meets with Kelleher every week to review current conditions in the market, scrutinize fares that the competition is advertising, and set strategy for keeping prices below everyone else's.

Although the company establishes some of its prices to coincide with special promotions, such as the $38 round-trip fare between Sacramento and Los Angeles in October 1995, other programs it originally developed for temporary use have survived for years. Its "Friends Fly Free" program, for example, was so popular that the airline continued it for five years. In 1996, Southwest introduced a replacement program called "Take Along," which allowed full-fare passengers on round-trip flights, excluding Orange County, to bring along as many as three companions for an additional $50 apiece. Using such promotions, the company establishes some of its pricing policies by taking account of its operating costs. Whether the plane is full or half-full, it still costs relatively the same amount (give or take a few gallons of diesel fuel) to fly from point A to point B. It stands to reason that selling a seat for $50 is better than allowing it to remain empty.

Given the demand for certain routes as well as the company's internal operating expenses, Southwest can factor in the variables—the prices offered by competitors in the air and on the ground, seasonal changes in the market, fuel costs, and the like—to calculate the lowest possible fare it can charge and still turn a profit. And those profits have soared to record heights: Southwest has shown a profit each year since 1973 and proclaims itself the airline that gave Americans the "freedom to fly."

Subprocess 3
Develop Advertising and
Promotion Strategies

Advertising and promotions are the first outreach to potential customers and as such should effectively position the company's image as well as its products and services. Advertising and promotion strategies, however, are not developed in a vacuum: Salespeople, marketers, engineers, product developers, public relations experts, and customer service reps all have a hand in creating the image that the public perceives.

A company can design its advertising and promotions to appeal directly to customers' needs and wants or to contrast its products with those of its competitors. Whatever its strategy, it should build a positive image and help potential customers recognize their need for the product or service. Once the company has identified those needs and segmented its market, as discussed in chapter 3, it can begin its advertising and promotion campaign. As important as the amount of money committed to the campaign is the need to track advertising to ensure that it is effective in reaching the target audience.

A world leader in designing advertising and promotion strategies, Nike illustrates how a best-practice company establishes an image and brings it into every home. Nike ads typically never even mention the product by name but rely instead on the "Swoosh" symbol or a well-known phrase such as "Just Do It" to do the selling. Its promotion spots acquire the status of celebrity interviews, entertaining as well as informing. As a result, Nike's audience is among the most loyal of customer segments.

NIKE, INC.

Great ads, by themselves, don't work. What does work, as Liz Dolan, vice president of marketing communications at Nike says, is "a combination of three essential ingredients: innovative products, focused segments, and a clear understanding of the emotional ties that bind customers to a particular sport." Nike's best practice underscores just how important it is for a company to form a total picture of its targeted customers so that everyone in the company—from product development to marketing—knows what products they want.

It's no secret that Nike has successfully promoted its products by creating images of world-class athletes such as Michael Jordan, Pete Sampras, and Jackie Joyner-Kersee, who seem to reach through the television screen to viewers, inviting them to join in the game. "Just Do It" is a phrase now known the world over. With immediate recognition value, the Nike "Swoosh," emblazoned on all its footwear and apparel, can now take the place of spoken or printed words in advertising the company.

A. Phil Knight, founder of Nike, commented in a recent article for *Harvard Business Review*, the company promotes images of world-class athletes at the peak of their abilities. "For years," Knight says, "we thought of ourselves as a production-oriented company, meaning we put all our emphasis on designing and manufacturing the product. But now we understand that the most important thing we do is market the product."

Nike's ads rarely detail the products themselves; in fact, they seldom mention specific design features such as type of sole or arch support. The company clearly recognizes that its core competence lies in utilizing its skills in marketing and advertising as well as product development. In an industry where several companies have established high levels of quality in footwear and apparel, what makes Nike stand out is the image of Air Jordan flying six feet above the floor for a slam dunk.

Nike's advertising agency, Wieden and Kennedy of Portland, Oregon, works with Nike to create winning campaigns such as the "Hare Jordan" ads featuring Michael Jordan and Bugs Bunny or the Penny Hardaway spots in which his brash alter ego "Little Penny" serves as a foil for the modest star.

Other Wieden and Kennedy ads appeal to specific groups such as young female athletes. The company long ago recognized a trend in modern American culture and elevated women's sports to a level they had never known before. Nike called this campaign "Just Let Me Play," a mantra that soon adorned T-shirts throughout the world. In addition, the company recently signed a five-year marketing contract with the Women's National Basketball Association and began plans to sponsor the Nike U.S. Cup tournament for international women's soccer teams.

Nike has masterfully read the signs of developing trends—the growing popularity of women's athletics, the astonishing rise of sports participants of every stripe and age since the 1970s—and the company has focused attention on what Liz Dolan calls the "soul" or *zeitgeist* of each sport: "What is it to play this game? What is it to love this game? What is the spirit of this sport?"

The answers to those questions, Dolan explains, are like pieces of a puzzle which, when fitted together, form a total picture that everyone in the company can see. Individually, those pieces comprise the strategies for product development, communications, and sports marketing. Nike begins the process of assembling this picture by creating cross-divisional "teams," each devoted to a specific sport. Team members—product developers, designers, marketers, public relations experts—spend time in the field observing and interviewing people playing that sport at all levels from preteens through the pros. (It doesn't hurt to have team members who are runners or basketball players themselves.)

As Dolan explains, the team members seek to discover what fires the public's imagination and devotion to a sport. Product designers and developers from each team then collaborate with that team's sports marketing person whose job it is to know the people who play that sport and to recommend the athletes the company should sign. A public relations expert works with the media outlets that cover that sport. The structure of the core marketing team for basketball, which is centered in the United States, may be quite different from that for soccer, which is based in Europe, with collaborating offices in Brazil and elsewhere; but the basic process is the same: Spend time in the field with the people who love and play the sport, then find a way to build a marketing strategy around that enthusiasm.

At Nike, the person responsible for translating this strategy into a business plan is usually the marketer, says Dolan. Aside from signing some of the greatest stars who have ever made jump shots at the buzzer or turned on the afterburner in a 200-meter sprint, Nike's forte continues to be a kind of applied psychology: the ability to know what motivates the kid on a playground or the middle-aged jogger preparing to enter next year's marathon, then to design marketing and advertising strategies infused with that spirit. At Nike the shoes must have souls.

Subprocess 4
Develop and Deploy a Sales Force

Traditionally in the United States and in many countries, salespeople have been paid on a commission basis with quotas geared to gross revenues and volume. As customers demand higher quality and more personal service, however, the focus of compensation is shifting to reward those employees who generate greater profits and customer satisfaction.

When aligned in teams rather than forced to compete as individuals, salespeople quickly adapt their behavior to address the increasing complexity of new products and to satisfy more demanding customers. In best-practice companies, managers discover that sales teams combine the varied skills of many employees and provide greater service than any one of them could offer singly. As equipment manufacturer Cutler-Hammer illustrates, the team-selling approach aligns salespeople with customers by company rather than by geography. The employee-customer relationship benefits when the members of the sales team are more familiar with a particular company's needs and can add value for the customer, often without charge. When a customer has multiple branches in various states or foreign countries, the benefits added for one branch can often be applied to all.

CUTLER-HAMMER

Supplying circuit breakers, motor starters, and other electrical equipment to heavy industrial manufacturers such as Ford Motor

Company, Pittsburgh-based Cutler-Hammer is a leader in the team-selling concept. As Bruce Broussard, currently commercial marketing manager for the component division of Cutler-Hammer, recalls, the idea met with skepticism, even ridicule, when it first came up in 1991. Dissatisfied with evaluating salespeople strictly on the basis of individual subjectivity, Broussard raised the issue with the sixteen salespeople of the Cincinnati unit he then managed: "We had never met as a team, so we had no way of working together. The only way we were treated as a team was in our pooled compensation. There were certain individuals who were landing multimillion-dollar projects. Others were sleeping until noon."

Gradually, the Cincinnati sales force took shape as a team, largely under the direction of Broussard and Doug Borchers, who was elected team leader. In response to the growing complexity and proliferation of its products, Cutler-Hammer developed "pods" of salespeople focused on a particular geographical region, industry, or market concentration. Each individual brought a degree of expertise about a product or service that the other members of the team could take to the customer. The old paradigm of each specialist calling on his or her favorite customers without bothering to learn how to leverage the knowledge of co-workers has largely been tossed into the bin of outmoded ideas.

In part, the team-selling approach has been a response to customer demand for specific solutions and expertise. Under the old paradigm, a sales representative might be familiar with a handful of products, none of which a particular customer needed at the time. Because products change so rapidly in the industrial equipment industry, sales reps found themselves struggling just to keep abreast of new product development. The new team-selling approach helps people share their knowledge, thereby coming up with solutions for customers much more effectively than any one salesperson could do before.

To initiate such a fundamental change in the corporate culture, Broussard led his colleagues through several team-building exercises. Team members examined their attitudes toward the new approach in games designed to enhance the spirit of cooperation. They also completed questionnaires and studied books on the team approach to selling. Schooled from their early years under a system of compensatory rewards for good behavior (that is, high sales), many members had to unlearn some old, unproductive habits. Cutler-Hammer's Quality Institute provided instruction in negotiating, value-added selling, conducting effective meetings, innovation and creativity, writing a mission statement, and linking the team's strategies to those of the company as a whole.

Changes in behavior have been extraordinary. "We went from zero testimonials," Broussard reports, "to creating a book of over 150 letters from customers saying why they do business with us. We developed an automated desktop publishing proposal process so that with a day's notice we can produce a binder customized for each customer, describing all the quality processes of our company, all the plant locations, everything pertinent to that customer, specifically to sell more of the big-picture corporate relationship. We created value-added no-charge invoices for service performed and a time line planning process to reduce sales cycle time, and celebrated our accomplishments regularly."

Those behavior changes represent a major ingredient in the team objective process utilized at Cutler-Hammer, which affected the sales engineers' merit pay increases. The company emphasizes the need to tie rewards to the process of customer satisfaction in addition to revenue growth. Most companies looking to the team-selling approach should think of the long-term value of customer relationships and satisfaction as well as the short-term revenue generated from sales.

This is what Cutler-Hammer has done. In a market that typically grows 4 percent to 7 percent a year, Broussard's team showed an outstanding annual growth of 18 percent over the period 1992 to 1995. Such results offer clear evidence of the value brought by the team approach.

Subprocess 5
Process Orders

Once a company has progressed through the steps of securing channels of distribution, establishing pricing, developing advertising strategies, and deploying its sales force, it should deliver the goods. This is done, first, by establishing a primary contact point for the customer to use in placing orders, resolving conflicts, and learning how to use the product or service it offers. This personal relationship affords the customer a knowledgeable individual to call on, an essential part in the building of company-client trust.

Out of this relationship can grow an integrated system for processing orders, one that is flexible and tailored to the individual customer's needs. Furthermore, that system should be linked to all of the customer's departments and locations so that its personnel can access inventory data when needed. An effective system captures pricing information, customer profiles, order history, current inventory, shipping information, and the like. The best of all possible systems does all this and never has to use the term "backordered."

Electronic data interchange (EDI) allows computers at one company to talk to those at a partner company. This technology has vastly transformed the ways that businesses communicate with each other, particularly in the areas of processing orders, invoicing, and fulfillment. A major distributor of health care products to hospitals and clinics, Allegiance Healthcare Corporation has made a best practice of this subprocess in marketing and selling its products and services.

ALLEGIANCE HEALTHCARE CORPORATION

Based in McGraw Park, Illinois, Allegiance Healthcare Corporation manufactures and distributes both its own surgical products and those of more than a thousand manufacturers worldwide. A spinoff of Baxter Healthcare Corporation, Allegiance first implemented its stockless inventory program known as "ValueLink" in 1988. Currently in service at over 150 acute-care hospitals in the United States, this program supplies hospital personnel with the products they need when they need them and where they are needed. Twenty customers in the rapidly expanding health care provider market outside of the hospital are already signed up as well (subacute surgery centers and other diagnostic and therapeutic care delivery sites).

Allegiance ships products to each facility in units of measurement that are ready for use in the customer's departments. In each of approximately a dozen hospitals, some 30 Allegiance employees are actually on the customer's premises full-time, 365 days a year, to hand-deliver products to emergency rooms, laboratories, and other areas.

Using the most sophisticated technology available, the ValueLink program achieves a fill rate in excess of 98 percent on the first shipment. Pricing accuracy is in the 99 percent range, much higher than a customer would likely expect when using several different suppliers. Allegiance attributes this accuracy to its cooperative customers and integrated EDI network, a flexible system for handling all orders and invoices electronically. According to Tony Kesman, corporate vice president of distribution at Allegiance, "About 96 percent of the order lines we receive from our customers now come through the EDI network. An equal amount of orders that we make to our suppliers are also handled electronically."

The key to Allegiance's success in processing orders is the integrated system that meets the needs of customers who are dealing with life-and-death situations every minute. In the traditional distribution system, an eighteen-wheeler simply dropped off a week's or even a month's worth of supplies at the back door of the hospital for central storage. As important items were used, there were various mechanisms for keeping track of the inventory. "We found out," says Kesman, "that the items in most demand often were the ones that the hospital was out of, whereas there were large quantities on hand of certain supplies they seldom needed. The caregiver, however, always had one thing on his or her mind relative to supplies: They wanted it on the shelf when they reached for it."

To design a new system, one that would provide the syringe when and where it was needed, Allegiance recognized the need to partner with its customers. For each prospective customer, the company undertakes a feasibility study that includes on-site interviews, data collection, needs assessment, and projections of trends. Once a customer decides to adopt the ValueLink program, an implementation team drives the process. A steering committee comprising both hospital employees and Allegiance personnel oversees the installation and assesses how effectively it is processing orders.

Allegiance estimates that the ValueLink system saves its customers an average of $500,000 or more each year. These savings come from improved replenishment processes, the consolidation of multiple vendors, and the reuse of space that is no longer needed to warehouse inventory for other hospital needs.

In providing a sophisticated inventory technology and working in close contact with each customer, Allegiance Healthcare has mastered the techniques of processing orders. The logical extension of this subprocess, as Allegiance so clearly recognizes, is product standardization. The company hires clinical project managers, often nurses or clinicians with business expertise, to observe the flow and consumption of materials. If a hospital is using three different types of catheters, for example, Allegiance suggests a single type that would work in any medical situation. As Kesman points out, "Our ability to standardize these items further creates value for our customers and simultaneously improves our productivity and returns. It's business-to-business marketing."

Subprocess 6
Develop Customers

Best-practice companies realize that they should target sales efforts and make them cost-effective. One way to drive down costs is to focus on well-qualified prospective customers, but converting those prospects into customers who pay their bills requires knowing as much about them as the company knows about its current customers. Savvy companies identify those customers they *want* to do business with, then devise a plan for cultivating those relationships and for closing sales.

As mass markets have given way to highly segmented ones, information about customers has become more important as a driver of marketing efforts. Sophisticated technology now makes it much easier to capture that information and to penetrate existing markets more deeply, as well as to make inroads into new markets.

A best-practice company gleans information from any interaction with a customer: Surveys, interviews, point-of-sale contact, repair calls, telephone or Internet inquiries, deliveries, and the like can bring in valuable data. As the example of Peapod, Inc., discussed earlier in this chapter, demonstrates, the very lifeblood of an organization flows along these channels of customer communication.

In addition, a company can use nonverbal methods to reach customers such as rebates, premium offers, and point-of-sale scanner technology. Outside databases can enrich this collection of customer information with geographic, demographic, and psychographic data.

Capturing customers that a company has lost or that currently belong to a competitor is one of the most challenging aspects of this subprocess. As mentioned in chapter 3, Fingerhut selects specific segments of its customers who have failed to repay loans but can show just cause for their delinquency. Rather than dismissing them as bad risks, the company invites those customers to make another purchase with Fingerhut. With its sophisticated customer profiles, Fingerhut can personally contact former customers, some of whom may have gone over to other companies, and offer to reinstate them as good credit risks.

Best-practice companies such as American Airlines and Enron Corp. excel in customer retention. They demonstrate reliable, consistent performance, credibility with their customers, responsiveness to customer demands, and personalized service. If a customer leaves a company, the shrewd manager will want to know why. The shrewder manager will ask, "What can we do to bring this customer back?"

The airline industry is blessed with a great supply of information about its customers: Patterns of travel, frequency of reservations, and method of payment are among the items recorded in the databases of all major airlines. In 1981, partly as a response to the deregulation of the industry, American Airlines recognized that it could harness this information and create a system that offered its best customers free tickets and other benefits. What is more, the company realized that its American AAdvantage plan could help guarantee customer loyalty as well as bring in the competition's customers who wanted better deals. "We started thinking about the lifetime value of customers as opposed to their transactional value," says Henry Joyner, vice president of marketing planning at American Airlines.

Originally designed to appeal to some half million of its business travelers, the American AAdvantage program now boasts over 29 million members worldwide, including a half million in Brazil alone. Since 1981, the company has partnered with the Hertz rental car agency and Hilton Hotels, and has since added other hotel and car rental companies as well as credit card services, mortgage companies, and even new car sales to attract customers seeking to build up their frequent flier miles. Over this period, American has followed three basic steps in the subprocess of developing customers for life:

1. It established key drivers of greater value and lower prices. After deregulation, American knew that customers would quickly develop a savvy about the industry's competitive structure and that the competition would be quick to imitate its frequent flier program. American's customers with E-mail addresses, for example, now receive weekly notices of heavily discounted NetsAAver fares.

2. It made current customers better customers by helping them learn how to take advantage of the frequent flier system and the company's partnerships with allied enterprises. If American contemplates a major schedule expansion, such as between Chicago and Los Angeles, it can contact in a direct mailing all its Los Angeles customers who have rented cars or hotel rooms in Chicago, informing them of the change so that they can preplan their travel accordingly.

3. It enticed customers away from the competition by improving on-time departure and arrival, increasing the number of AAdvantage member services, delivering more benefits through its AAdvantage Gold program, introduced in 1983, and establishing its own AAdvantage credit card in 1987.

ENRON CORP.

When most customers think of the gas and electric power industry, they think of big centralized power plants, those behemoths called public utilities, monopolies that have ruled the industry for the past century. As Jeffrey Skilling, president and COO of Enron, testified in March 1997 before a Senate committee on energy and natural resources, "No one can seriously defend that system anymore. It is inefficient. It is unnecessarily costly. It stifles innovation. It forces consumers to pay high rates while large industrial customers get special rates."

Changes in the energy industry began gradually in the early 1980s when the deregulation of wholesalers allowed for more competition in the energy market. Now that deregulation is reaching all the way down to individual end users, smaller members in the industry are poised to leapfrog over the behemoths by educating customers, one house or business at a time, to understand the choices that will transform the way they think about energy.

Voted "most innovative company in the United States" by its competitors in *Fortune* magazine's 1996 and 1997 surveys of America's most admired companies, Enron Corp. is a diversified energy company operating across North America and overseas. The company recognizes that the number of its potential energy customers will skyrocket from perhaps ten thousand today to as many as 120 million in ten years. The primary driver of this sharp increase is deregulation: As Skilling points out, "Customers will ultimately be able to choose who their gas and electricity supplier is. Enron can then enter a neighborhood or an individual house and educate residents on the cheapest way of providing high-quality energy." It may be something as simple, Skilling explains, as putting a solar panel on the roof of a suburban home or installing a microturbine atop a fast-food restaurant, then providing the natural gas to power the machine to convert the energy into electricity on the spot. In either case, Enron has to educate potential customers about the wealth of choices already available to them. In doing so, the company engages in the subprocess of developing customers.

"Right now, when you move into a new area," says Skilling, "you call up the utility company and order your energy. They don't ask you what you want. They just give it to you."

Whether for this individual homeowner or a large consortium of companies such as the New York State Restaurant Association, Enron understands the key drivers that either convert prospects into customers or target competitors' customers. In the newly deregulated natural gas and electricity industry, those drivers are accessibility, costs, availability, and service. Most energy consumers in the United States, Skilling told the Senate committee, do not realize that "wholesale electricity sells for, on average, two cents per kilowatt hour, yet consumers pay anywhere from three to eight times that amount."

Enron Corp. is committed to developing customers in this newly emerging marketplace. Only a few years ago the company had almost no one to perform the function of educating potential customers, but now a force of nearly one thousand employees handles this task. That's a best practice.

BEST-PRACTICE AGENDA

Make sure you know all links in your value chain—all suppliers, distributors, advertisers, marketers, salespeople, and customers. By its thorough understanding of its value chain, Lexus was able to overcome potential distribution problems.

Establish a competitive pricing strategy, as Southwest Airlines has done by looking outside its industry (namely, to automobile rentals and other modes of transportation) to determine pricing policies.

Develop strong advertising strategies, seeking input from all levels of your company to develop an appropriate image that can distinguish your company from others in the industry. As Nike has proven, developing a good product is only half the battle. You also have to get the message to your customers.

Train your employees, especially those who will sell your products and services, to know everything they need to know about the market, the item they are selling, and the customers to whom they are selling. As Cutler-Hammer illustrates with its team-selling approach, this melding of individuals with different talents and degrees of expertise makes good business sense.

Develop an integrated system for processing orders tailored to customers' needs. Through its ValueLink program, Allegiance Healthcare serves over 150 acute-care hospitals in the United States with 98 percent fill-rate accuracy.

Do business with the customers you choose and in the ways you choose—by surveys, interviews, point-of-sale contacts, repair calls, and the like. As Peapod, Inc., and American Airlines have demonstrated, it is possible to partner with customers, establishing key drivers of greater value and lower prices.

Top Ten Best Practice Diagnostic Questions

1. The foundation of a successful sales effort is knowledge of customer needs and an ability to communicate how your products and services best fit those needs. What training systems does your company use to educate your salespeople and service technicians on (1) identifying customers' key needs and (2) differentiating your products and services from those of the competition?

2. How often do you retrain your employees in these and other areas? What tests do you give them?

3. When was the last time you critically evaluated your channels of distribution? Have you considered emerging channels such as the Internet?

4. Do you monitor your price performance and that of your competitors? How do you determine what customers are willing to pay?

5. Does your advertising strategy address current and developing trends in your market?

6. Have you studied non-customers and your lost customers to identify their needs? Have you responded to them appropriately?

7. How do you go about building a positive image for your company and its products? How do you help potential customers understand that they need your products and services?

8. What degree of integration (such as EDI) do you have in place for processing orders?

9. What special offers or incentives do you offer selected segments of your customers?

10. Do you know what differentiates your products and services from your competitors' products and services? How do you communicate those differences?

CHAPTER 6

LET THE BUYER BE AWARE

How to Involve Customers in Product Delivery

SUBPROCESSES

Offer Broad Delivery Options to Become the "Supplier of Choice"

Use Delivery Customization to Attract and Retain Core Customers

Identify Customers' Delivery Needs

Develop Distribution Capability

BEST-PRACTICE COMPANIES

Allegiance Healthcare

Holy Cross Hospital

New Pig

Norrell

SARCOM

Granite Rock Company

Cemex S.A. de C.V. (Cemex)

Campbell Soup Company

Not all companies deal in life-and-death situations where a delay in delivery results in something much more serious than an irritated customer. As we saw in the previous chapter, however, Illinois-based Allegiance Healthcare has made it one of its best practices to respond to its customers' needs in emergency situations. Through its ValueLink program, it has become the largest supplier in the United States of medical, surgical, and laboratory products. Not only does it manufacture many of those products itself, but it also distributes those of over a thousand other companies to hospitals and medical institutions throughout the country. A spinoff of Baxter Healthcare Corporation, Allegiance now concentrates on distribution and cost-management services for acute care facilities.

Like many other best-practice companies, Allegiance targets low costs, high-quality standards, and quick responsiveness to its customers' needs. The company produces what customers want, when they need it; nothing else matters.

Best-practice companies learn that involving their customers effectively in the delivery of products and services takes mastering four basic subprocesses: They should (1) aggressively pursue options to become the "supplier of choice," (2) offer core clients realistic customization of delivery and supply options, (3) identify each customer's individual delivery needs, and (4) develop the best capabilities for distributing products and services.

Partnering with its suppliers and customers, Allegiance improves its forecasting and minimizes costly mistakes by creating a fast, flexible delivery system. It has accomplished this feat by means of just-in-time supply and replenishment services. As mentioned in chapter 5, Allegiance can deliver medical supplies not just to a hospital's loading dock but to a specific unit within the facility where those products are needed. In typical supplier-customer relationships, each side works independently in maintaining inventories, streamlining production, finding efficient delivery systems, and reducing overall costs. As Allegiance demonstrates, however, this traditional relationship is no longer good enough. In order to be competitive, suppliers and customers should work together to find ways to meet customers' needs.

Allegiance has discovered that developing a sense of trust with a customer is key to becoming its supplier of choice. Committed to common goals, both supplier and customer create a seamless operation dedicated to delivering products efficiently and economically. As an emerging trend in that relationship, the supplier arranges with a customer to locate an "in-plant" representative at the customer's site on a full- or part-time basis. Allegiance, for example, now has over 300 in-plants in several hospitals operated by its biggest customers. With access to customers' inventory systems, those in-plants can create, adjust, cancel, and expedite orders. In essence, they replace the sales representative and assist in keeping production on track. On-site suppliers can also interact with customers to streamline production, whether the care of a patient or the creation of a prototype is at stake. In this new business environment, logistics takes on increasing significance: Trucking, shipping, billing, and communications at every level become integrated for both parties.

Such arrangements are mutually beneficial: Suppliers can achieve deep sales and service level penetration and the ready advantage to pursue new opportunities as they arise; customers can reduce overhead costs by purchasing fewer materials and reducing their staffs. With improved communications attributable to supplier in-plants, both sides can lower their operating costs and engage in more creative problem solving.

In some partnering hospitals, Allegiance has installed automatic dispensing devices. A user punches in a customer code and receives a syringe, a catheter, or whatever product is needed for a patient's care. The machine keeps track of each transaction, bills the customer immediately for the product, and generates a replenishment order for Allegiance to fill. This high degree of customization demonstrates the full extent to which creative partnerships can lead.

In order to achieve this customization, Allegiance seeks constant feedback from its customers on how the system meets their needs. The hospital does incur the cost for the dispensing system but no longer needs to employ someone to go to different units, gathering products and placing orders for new ones.

As a best-practice company, Allegiance continues to demonstrate its thorough understanding of its customers' delivery requirements. Whether an enterprise produces automobiles or treats cancer patients, its suppliers have to know the impact their deliveries have on that customer's ability to produce and deliver its own products and services. To this end, in-depth customer profiles need to include such details as warehouse limitations, reordering and delivery tracking systems, and customers' protocols for receipt of goods. Those protocols can change the delivery channel strategy at any time. If Allegiance partners with a large trauma care center, that customer's needs may sometimes take precedence over those of other facilities.

Allegiance Healthcare has developed its distribution capability by aligning its strategies so that they serve the needs of its hospital customers. It has integrated downstream partnerships to increase both efficiency and effectiveness, thereby offering its core customers greater value for their dollar. Integrating delivery with marketing and manufacturing, for instance, boosts overall efficiency for both sides. To build such partnerships requires trust, openness to change, and the willingness to share in the gains.

As the seven companies featured in this chapter demonstrate, close attention to improving distribution and delivery systems is essential in developing and maintaining lasting symbiotic relationships between customer and supplier. For companies wanting to involve their customers in the delivery of their products and services, the first step is to differentiate themselves from their competitors, thereby becoming the supplier of choice.

Subprocess 1
Offer Broad Delivery Options to Become the "Supplier of Choice"

In today's competitive environment, customers look beyond the simple formation of alliances with a strategic supplier; instead, customers seek the supplier who has the greatest stake in their mutual success. At the same time, suppliers strive to build equity with their customers by becoming an integral part of their core customers' business operations. In short, these companies strive to become the *suppliers of choice.*

In these new relationships, trust underlies the success of the venture. Particularly when two or more companies share their confidential information, people from both sides learn to respect each other's business values and practices. Whether a company achieves its supplier-of-choice status by means of an "in-plant representative" or EDI, the key is to establish a presence in the customer's business environment.

To become the supplier of choice, best-practice companies are also transforming their delivery strategies beyond the mere transportation of goods. They now include inventory management, product assembly, and sometimes even "resident suppliers" who work at the customer's site to oversee the distribution of products.

In evaluating the options for establishing a supplier-of-choice relationship, the best-practice company may decide to extend its current offerings by expanding its distribution channels to reach new customers. For example, Norrell Corporation, a major agency for placing temporary workers, has broadened its range of personnel to better satisfy the needs of its customers in an increasingly diverse market. A best-practice company may also attempt to seal off a market from competitors by improving its existing products and tightening the lines of distribution, just as the New Pig Corporation has done with contained absorbents used to clean up industrial spills and other contaminants. And as Holy Cross Hospital demonstrates, a best-practice company can often enhance its delivery capabilities of services at the same time that it works with customers to make existing services better.

Holy Cross Hospital

In 1991, Holy Cross Hospital in Chicago lost $9 million and was ranked in the bottom 5 percent of health care facilities in the United States, as measured by the Press-Ganey Patient Satisfaction index of approximately 440 hospitals nationwide. Even the staff at Holy Cross went somewhere else for their health care needs, and several employees said they were too embarrassed even to acknowledge that they worked at the hospital.

Conditions took a dramatic turn in September 1992 when new CEO Mark Clement arrived and the hospital's managers began a concerted effort to become the "provider of choice" for residents on Chicago's south side. As Liz Jazwiec, former acting vice president of nursing, reports, the hospital jumped 80 percentile points in the Press-Ganey survey—from 14 to 94—between October 1993 and July 1994. Today, rather than being shunned by patients and staff, the hospital attracts many admirers, among them over two hundred other hospitals that have gone to Chicago to study the best practices that Holy Cross Hospital has initiated.

Much of the credit for this turnaround goes to Clement, who built a sense of trust among staff and patients. He clarified the hospital's five core standards—service, excellence, respect, value, and enthusiasm—through the acronym SERVE and offered his own example as a model of dedication. Patients can call him directly if they feel dissatisfied with any part of the service they receive at Holy Cross Hospital.

But one person does not move an entire hospital up 80 points in a patient satisfaction survey in a single year. That accomplishment belongs to the fifteen hundred staff members, now called "partners," each of whom participates in the service delivery that distinguishes Holy Cross Hospital as a best-practice institution. Thanks to input from both partners and patients, the hospital has improved its service offerings even down to the smallest detail: Metal X-ray tables are now heated with electric blankets before patients lie down on them, and the hospital has altered its hours of operation as well as its policies regulating the number of visitors permitted in a room—all at the requests of the customers it serves.

All Holy Cross patients are asked to complete a questionnaire and rank the hospital's services, everything from the quality of the food to the treatment in the intensive care unit. Based on their customers' responses, partners identify specific irritants or barriers to patient satisfaction. They then hand this list over to a "commando team" whose sole reason for existence is to make the patient's hospital experience as near perfect as possible. Armed with specific requests from customers, these commandos have "zapped" over a hundred irritations. The staff in the imaging department, for example, must acknowledge a patient within one minute of arrival and cannot keep that customer waiting longer than ten minutes. Nurses on daily rounds must explain any test scheduled for a patient and provide written descriptions when appropriate. The hospital even provides valet parking.

Central to its goal of becoming the hospital of choice for residents in south Chicago, Holy Cross undertook a program of developing medical affiliates in neighborhoods where none existed. According to Jazwiec, "We understood that if we were going to remain financially viable, we had to recruit physicians who would be willing to practice in our neighborhood." When the program started, the Marquette Park community, for example, had no practicing pediatricians; now there are eight on staff at the hospital. Patients at any affiliated clinic have direct access to the hospital for immediate admission and treatment.

For eight consecutive quarters Holy Cross Hospital achieved a score in the 98th percentile or higher according to the Press-Ganey index, and in 1996, it was ranked the sixth best hospital in the United States. Outstanding results such as these qualify Holy Cross as a best-practice company that has achieved its improvements by involving its customers directly in the delivery of services.

New Pig Corporation

Combining a great sense of humor and smart business practices, the New Pig Corporation produces and markets absorbents for cleaning up industrial spills and wastes. In 1985, the company invented an absorbent sock it called the "Pig," which became so popular that it quickly replaced the traditional method of throwing clay particles on a spill or leak. Recognizing a winning product, the company considered changing its name from Sermac to the Pig Corporation as a result, but finding that name already taken, chose New Pig instead. Chuckles have come ever since, and the company continues to generate smiles with marketing innovations such as snout hats that oink, its toll-free customer service number 1-800-HOTHOGS, and its upscale address of One Pork Avenue in Tipton, Pennsylvania.

According to Nino Vella, president and CEO of New Pig, the company is both market-driven and product-driven. "Right from the start," Vella says, "we defined customer service, warehousing, fulfillment, and MIS as functions that supported marketing and the customer, not necessarily finance or operations. That was the key in getting us to where we are today."

The free-squealing culture at New Pig is one that encourages a constant stream of new ideas. Many of these are generated in-house, of course, but Vella knows the importance that customer and supplier input can have on product development. With this in mind, customer service calls at the company are often monitored by New Pig executives, who work with the phone reps to cull useful information from every call. Long after becoming president, Vella himself undertook customer service training and began taking customer calls to get a better understanding of the process.

"We've designed an ideal for customer service, and we've designed to fit that ideal," he explains. "Instead of looking at a customer complaint and thinking, 'Oh, no, here's another jerk,' we should think, 'What can we learn from this, and how can we use it to serve this customer better or make a better product?'"

Vella believes in taking his customers' advice seriously. "We found out," he says, "that our customers hate back orders. So we engineered back orders out of our company." How did New Pig accomplish this feat? It ignored conventional wisdom about inventory management and decided to spend approximately

$300,000 annually to keep its inventory stocked at a minimum of 99 percent of capacity. That way, even the one customer who orders a specialized product that otherwise gathers dust on the shelf is never disappointed. "We felt that having the excess inventory was more important for our customers than the $300,000 savings. In the end, we more than make that up by continuing to have good customer relations," says Vella.

Such practices in distribution afford New Pig many opportunities to build working partnerships with its customers. Vella is orchestrating a company-wide effort to become the supplier of choice for customers. To accomplish this goal, the company has created the PIT, a database of over 4,000 customer suggestions, complaints, and ideas that are not only made available to everyone in the New Pig organization but also channeled immediately to the most appropriate person or department that can solve the problem.

In addition, the company offers same-day shipping, an essential service when a customer faces a major disaster such as a dangerous chemical spill. Confident in the quality of what it sells, New Pig has a lifetime, money-back guarantee on each of its 3500 products. It provides 24-hour assistance for customers to contact the company regarding orders or technical support both by phone and by modem.

But the customer service does not stop there. One evening Betty Narehood received an emergency call at New Pig's corporate headquarters in Tipton. A customer specializing in hazardous materials had reported a major fire at its plant. It was too late to save the plant, but according to state law, the customer was still responsible for cleaning up the hazardous materials within 24 hours. Narehood recognized that this request called for immediate action.

She assembled an interdepartmental team to override internal ordering and shipping protocols. This team put together an order of absorbents and called a local shipper. Because no commercial trucking company was available at that late hour, one of Narehood's colleagues volunteered, on his own time, to drive a New Pig truck to the customer some four hours away.

This kind of behavior is typical of employees at New Pig Corporation where "taking care of business" means "taking care of customers." Such practices increase customer loyalty and continue to ensure that New Pig remains the supplier of choice. Indeed, the company's annual sales now top $70 million, due in part to its stellar relationships with its customers.

"With us, a customer gets an extraordinary experience and a superb product," says Carl DeCaspers, manager of public relations. "We differentiate ourselves from our competitors by going that extra mile, whether it's by keeping our warehouse fully stocked, by servicing customers with the technical support they need, or by responding individually to any customer's emergency, even if that call comes late in the night."

NORRELL CORPORATION

In 1990, Atlanta-based Norrell Corporation recognized that the market for temporary staffing was at a standstill due to the down economy. Norrell conducted a survey of a thousand current and potential customers, who told the company what it did *not* want to hear: No one could differentiate it from scores of other temp agencies.

Becoming the supplier of choice in a market where there is little differentiation between competitors presented Norrell managers with a Herculean task, but they were determined to make their company the nation's top provider of temporary staffing. "Out of this survey we saw an opportunity to become the recognized highest-quality player in our industry segment," says Doug Miller, Norrell's president and CEO. To differentiate Norrell, Miller realized that strong customer service was not enough. The company needed to supply its clients with temporary personnel who stood head and shoulders above the employees furnished by competitors. "If you aren't providing quality people who are better equipped to do the job of boosting productivity, your customers are not going to perceive you as being any better than the rest."

After collecting data from the initial thousand customers regarding what they wanted in temporary personnel, Norrell was able to identify its customers' demands for excellence in the following areas: punctuality, productivity, job skills, attitude, attire, communication skills, employee preparation, adherence to safety instructions (for industrial employees), and branch responsiveness. In order to achieve its goal of becoming North America's highest-quality staffing company, Norrell developed IRIS (integrated research information system), an automated method by which to measure its service against customer expectations and improve it.

A one-of-a-kind quality measurement tool, IRIS generates a survey after each assignment to measure the Norrell employee on a scale of one to five in ten dimensions of quality. A central database at the company's corporate offices scans the feedback from customers and generates reports measuring quality by branch, customer, and employee. (The survey response rate is over 40 percent.) Managers then use the feedback to evaluate, reward, and counsel employees according to their performance. In addition to improving customer service, Norrell compensates its employees and recognizes its branch teams for improvements to their quality scores.

An important way that Norrell increases productivity and service quality is through accurate placement of skilled employees.

To promote this competitive advantage, the company developed its Exact Match Program, a process to recruit, assess, screen, interview, and match temporary employees with each customer, and then inform that customer about the employees' qualifications. Through this six-step process, Norrell meets the challenge of becoming the supplier of choice. The company recruits, on average, some five thousand potential employees a day, and their qualifications are entered into the Norrell database for future exact matches. As Kent Smith, CIO at Norrell, explains, "We look at ten or twelve possible ways we can go wrong in assessing an individual. That's sixty thousand potential fail points a day in matching an individual with one of our clients."

Norrell now implements a highly selective recruitment process whereby it interviews up to 20 people for a single position, a huge increase from the traditional industry standard of 5:1. It places 50,000 of its employees every day in temporary jobs; many of them work up to 90 days at the host company.

In order to better serve those large customers who prefer to deal with fewer vendors and choose a single preferred provider, Norrell has also developed its Master Vendor Partnership (MVP) program, wherein it acts as general manager for all of a customer's staffing needs. Norrell currently has in-depth MVP relationships with approximately 80 companies among its hundreds of clients, including North American–wide arrangements with the likes of Prudential and IBM. Those 80 companies account for 40 percent of Norrell's revenues and, in 1996 alone, employed more than one-quarter of its 220,000 temporary employees.

"With MVP we become the exclusive manager of that process," explains Smith. "We will supply the majority of our clients' needs directly or, if we cannot meet them, subcontract them to another supplier. Our focus on the customer led us into strategic workforce management, whereby we provide the thinking and planning, and accept overall responsibility for the quality of our people and the services they provide."

Subprocess 2
Use Delivery Customization to Attract and Retain Core Customers

As discussed in chapter 5, many best-practice companies have turned their attention to customizing products and services for particular customers in an effort to become the supplier of choice. Customization, however, can occur in packaging and delivery systems as well. A successful approach to customization focuses on those attributes that core customers value most and that the company can do best.

Customer-supplier communications lie at the base of this subprocess. Direct communication allows experts from both sides to resolve problems of distribution and delivery quickly and efficiently. Involving the customer helps promote a sense of ownership in the solution to the problem. Shortening the lines of communication inevitably leads to a quicker response and better-served customers.

Best-practice companies obtain constant customer feedback to make sure customer needs are being met. Furthermore, as discussed later in this chapter, SARCOM has developed its CERRFS program to customize the delivery of products and services to its customers. By maintaining constant communication with customers before, during, and after the problem is addressed, SARCOM technicians and salespeople are ready at any time to help steer expectations and involve customers in the delivery process.

SARCOM

Headquartered in Columbus, Ohio, SARCOM helps large companies implement information technology by providing computers, consulting, training, a help desk, outsourcing, and a variety of other support systems. In the business of reselling and repairing computer systems, however, there is little to distinguish SARCOM from other companies in terms of prices and products.

As its president Randy Wilcox says, "If you purchase a computer from SARCOM, it's the same exact computer that my competitor can sell you. Back in 1987, we were trying to determine what we could do to differentiate our products and services from those of our competitors, to gain a sustainable competitive advantage. We knew we could not have a major price or product advantage."

That year, Wilcox instituted a significant change in the company's corporate culture, directing employees to become totally focused on taking care of customers' needs. He developed an ongoing series of monthly meetings, mandatory for all employees at each of the company's branches, to discuss how to improve their efforts to satisfy customers. Wilcox himself conducted every meeting at each branch through 1996 and now attends one per branch each quarter.

Wilcox observed at those meetings that generally the same employees were winning all the company's awards for outstanding customer service. When he asked the winners for their secret, he discovered that all of them were following the same basic steps to satisfying customers. "The amazing thing," says Wilcox, "is that at every office I went to, I heard the same thing: Four of the six steps to success had to do with communication, not with fixing the technical problem."

Out of this survey grew the concept of CERRFS, an acronym

Wilcox developed to systematize the approach for all employees. This six-step process places the appropriate emphasis on communicating with the customer and clarifying expectations both before and after a problem is solved. The six steps are:

1. Call the customer and review the problem.
2. Expectation: Clearly set the expectation level for the customer as to what will happen next.
3. Restate the problem, once you arrive, to ensure you understand it. Have the customer show you the problem.
4. Restate expectations.
5. Fix the problem.
6. Show the customer what you did to fix the problem and ask if he or she is satisfied.

The next step in Wilcox's plan was to inscribe the six steps on plastic cards and give one to each employee to memorize. Whereas in the past a technician would merely have shown up at a customer's office to fix a problem, now the technician must call first to discuss the situation with the customer. "I understand that you have a problem with your computer. I think I may know what's wrong, but why don't you describe the problem to me."

Next, the technician sets proper expectations for the customer about possible solutions. According to Wilcox, this is probably the most important step because incorrect expectations lay the foundation for later disappointment. The SARCOM employee also estimates the time he or she will arrive at the customer's location. Once at the site, the technician asks the customer to restate the problem, preferably with a hands-on demonstration. This allows the technician to totally understand the nature of the problem.

At this point the SARCOM technician resets the expectations for the customer and begins fixing the problem. After finishing the project, the technician presents in detail the solution and how it was accomplished, again allowing the customer to ask questions, make further suggestions, or discuss additional issues.

"No matter how good our employees are technically, they cannot accomplish our goals if they can't follow these six steps and make the customer happy," says Wilcox. "They're not there just to fix the problem. They're there to fix the customer!"

Today, more than 1,400 SARCOM professionals in fifteen major cities find solutions for their customers in such varied industries as retail, banking, food service, public utilities, and telecommunications. Monthly surveys of its customers tell SARCOM how its products and services are received. When problems do arise, all SARCOM employees are empowered by the company to spend up to $500—no questions asked—to solve a customer problem. "I don't care what it costs," says Wilcox, "and we don't even track it. I know the alternative of losing a customer is much more expensive, and we've lost only two in the last seven or eight years."

Subprocess 3
Identify Customers' Delivery Needs

The only rule in delivering products and services to customers is to make sure they get what they need when they need it. If a company fails to understand how its delivery service affects its customers' business, it will miss opportunities to streamline the distribution process and capture a greater share of the market. The company that cannot or will not align its delivery processes to customers' needs unnecessarily drives up costs for both parties.

The two best-practice companies highlighted under this subprocess—Granite Rock Company and Cemex S.A. de C.V. (Cemex)—deal with industrial construction materials, but the two commodities handlers differ markedly in the problems they have had to address to meet customers' needs. Neither company has shied away from heavy investments in EDI and other technological systems to enhance their distribution processes. As best-practice companies they exemplify the benefits that come with a full understanding of the customer's business and delivery needs.

GRANITE ROCK COMPANY

In California, renting trucks to move large quantities of construction materials can cost a dollar or more a minute. To cut time and costs, construction companies constantly seek faster means of loading and transporting materials to their sites. Through its surveys, Granite Rock Company of Watsonville, California, discovered that its customers, large construction companies, were primarily concerned with the quick unloading of materials. Time, especially in the construction industry, is money.

Granite Rock set up a monitoring system to determine exactly how long it took a truck driver to enter one of its quarries, accept a load of rock or sand (not to exceed 80,000 pounds gross, the maximum weight permitted by California law), receive a sales tag, and get back on the road. To their surprise, managers at Granite Rock found the process consumed 24 minutes; even worse, trucks left the site an average of 800 pounds underweight. As Bruce Woolpert, president and CEO of Granite Rock, explains, "A contractor had to be thinking, 'I've been shorted almost half a ton.' After all, if trucks are under the 80,000-pound limit, the customers are not getting their full value for their trucking dollars. We even sat outside some of our competitors' gates and timed them. Although we were slightly faster than they were, three or four minutes are not a big advantage if you've already been waiting almost a half hour."

Woolpert and his staff determined the company had two primary problems: how to store materials prior to loading and how to find a fast, accurate electronic loading system that could accommodate materials of varying density. Because some materials flow faster than others, the company had to design a system that could be customized to open or close loading gates at various intervals depending on the material.

During a meeting with its banking partner, a Granite Rock quarry operator convinced the staff that the company should adopt a system similar to an ATM machine, one that would accept an identification card, authorize the release of materials to the user, and print a receipt. Because of dusty conditions at the quarry, the company decided to adapt the bank's ATM system by installing a radio frequency technology that would permit a trucker simply to point the identification card at a monitoring device to register the transaction. To achieve this best-practice accessibility, the company invested only about $300,000 in software and hardware for the GraniteXpress system and $3 million to upgrade the loading facility at its A. R. Wilson Quarry.

As part of the new delivery process, it also installed 120 pull cords that run the entire length of the loading area, so that wherever truckers load, they have easy access to control the process, including emergency stops. The GraniteXpress system further provides 24-hour-a-day delivery, seven days a week, thus allowing truckers the opportunity to set their own schedules for pickup. As Woolpert says, "The drivers wanted control, so we gave them control. If they want to move at night, when there's less traffic, now they can."

In 1992, Granite Rock Company won the Malcolm Baldrige National Quality Award in the category of small businesses. The company continues to track the effectiveness of its delivery system, which initially cut time of delivery in half. With further improvements, the company has reduced the loading time to a mere seven minutes. According to Woolpert, "That's saving seventeen minutes or seventeen dollars for every load that goes through, a significant savings for our customers."

Deregulation in the California trucking system in 1995 made it more difficult for companies to rent large numbers of trucks. Thus, it is now increasingly important for a customer to make effective use of available vehicles. Because of its understanding of customers' delivery requirements, Granite Rock has doubled its market share since 1989, thanks in large part to GraniteXpress.

CEMEX S.A. DE C.V. (CEMEX)

Founded in 1906 and based in Monterrey, Mexico, Cemex is the largest producer of cement in the Americas and the third largest in the world. The company has operations in more than 20 countries and trade relations in more than 60 countries. It is the top producer of cement in Mexico, Spain, Panama, Venezuela, and the Dominican Republic, and has significant operations in Colombia and the southwestern United States. In order to keep tabs on hundreds of delivery vehicles, numerous shipping lines, and over twenty thousand employees, management decided in 1988 to install a sophisticated high-technology solution that links dispatchers, truckers, and customers by satellites, computers, and modems.

Customers demand that cement deliveries be on time, and Cemexnet, the company's domestic Information Technology (IT) system, allows the company to reach almost perfect order fulfillment. In its Venezuelan operation, which is described as low-tech, Cemex achieved an on-time delivery rate of just over 33 percent in the first half of March 1996 (nearly 60 percent were delivered "ahead" of time). In contrast, the Guadalajara operations achieved a 98 percent on-time delivery rate during the same period, as

Wired magazine reported recently (July 1997). The difference lies in the new integrated system, which receives and processes orders as well as tracks delivery vehicles through the maze of streets and construction sites.

In the construction industry, where an hour's delay of a delivery can force a customer's crew to stop work entirely, Cemex knows that it cannot afford to ignore the impact that deliveries have on its customers. When someone phones in an order to the company, that message can appear on a truck driver's monitor specifying exactly where and when the delivery is to be made. If a delay occurs at the construction site, however, a customer can request that the shipment be postponed, and Cemex can respond in an instant to alter its delivery schedule accordingly. In essence, Cemex treats its trucks like taxicabs by dispatching the closest vehicle to the most immediate need. After all, cement is cement. It does not matter which truck delivers it.

Whether in regard to a business unit's strategic goals or the efficiency of a specific truck, Cemex's global technology system gives the company real-time, online information that it can share with employees and customers. Its thorough understanding of customers' requirements and its ability to coordinate deliveries have led to Cemex's being recognized by *Computerworld* magazine in its list of the one hundred most outstanding users of information technology at the global level.

Subprocess 4
Develop Distribution Capability

Once a company develops a deep understanding of its customers' delivery needs, it should form a distribution capability designed with those customers in mind. First, it should align its delivery strategies to service specific customer segments. Second, it should integrate that delivery process with all other functions such as marketing, product development, sales, and customer service. In addition to this internal integration, the company should form downstream partnerships whenever possible to supply maximum value to customers. If the company cannot deliver the goods on time, it needs to find a partner who will. Finally, the best-practice company should constantly evaluate the delivery process and the effectiveness of its partnerships, making changes where appropriate to ensure the rapid, responsive, and reliable delivery of its products and services. Venerable Campbell Soup Company, already a market leader in production, has become a best-practice company in the area of delivering its goods to customers. Since incorporating these changes, Campbell's has reduced shipping costs by over 10 percent and made it easier to track shipments.

CAMPBELL SOUP COMPANY

Founded in 1869 in Camden, New Jersey, the Campbell Soup Company became a household word for brands that customers cannot do without. Everyone, of course, knows what "M'm! M'm! Good!" means, but Campbell's products include more than the famous soups. The company also produces V8 vegetable juice, Swanson frozen dinners, Vlasic pickles, Godiva chocolates, Pepperidge Farm bakery goods, Franco-American canned pastas, and numerous other items.

Over the last few years the company undertook several initiatives to eliminate non-value-added costs in its supply chain and to create greater value for its customers. As Sally Schukraft, vice president of sales services, puts it, "We concluded that the industry was passing us by and that the salespeople could not continue to do their job based on great brands alone. We needed to create a multifunctional team to address the customer's needs."

Although its on-time delivery was already at 98 percent, Campbell's saw the opportunity to make major improvements in its distribution system. These were aimed at reducing paperwork, preventing damage to goods, and helping many of its customers save money by ordering goods directly from a Campbell's manufacturing plant.

Before the changes, the company was awash in paperwork generated by dealings with more than 300 carriers servicing 24 autonomous shipping locations. All told, shipments added up to over 197,000 per year. The operation was so manual in nature that to check on the status of a delivery, various people at each plant would have to call each customer. Because communications within this network were so unwieldy, Campbell's found that on-time deliveries suffered when third-party trucks broke down or drivers failed to secure a delivery appointment.

Under the leadership of CEO David Johnson, however, the company initiated numerous improvements in its distribution capability. Specifically, Campbell's managers set out to follow a four-step process:

1. Alignment of delivery strategies.

2. Integration of those strategies with the company's functional operations and with particular customers by reducing paperwork and creating a centralized customer service center.

3. Development and integration of downstream partnerships for fast, accurate distribution.

4. Evaluation and streamlining of those partnerships for continuous replenishment and improved performance.

Alignment of Delivery Strategies

According to Dave Thompson, vice president of distribution logistics at Campbell's, "We used to have orders originating in all of our sales regions. We had transportation being done at each of the plants. The cash application and the credit collection was done back in Camden. To streamline this process, we brought all those functions together in one centralized location, aligning sales and customer service under the auspices of a team assigned to each major customer."

Since the establishment of a centralized customer service center near Campbell's headquarters, each customer now works with a specified contact person for what Schukraft calls "one-stop shopping." Using the new system, a customer can check on the status of an order, change an order, or reschedule a delivery time with a single phone call.

Integration of Delivery Operations

Using electronic transmission, Campbell's central customer service center monitors the progress of goods from distribution points to the final destination. Before the installation of this system, Campbell's experienced a lot of "dead time," both at the point of origin and at the destination when the schedule for loading and unloading trucks was interrupted. Rather than loading a truck at 9:00 A.M., waiting several hours, and then driving it away at 4:00 P.M., the new system utilizes paperless EDI technology to ensure that the shipping department will begin loading precisely on schedule with the truck's departure to eliminate dead time and costly delays. The system then continues to track that shipment and reports overages, shortages, and damages at the customer's unloading site. Noting any damage or unfulfilled orders, the system creates a streamlined and efficient network for integrating the delivery process with customers.

Campbell's employs statistical process control (SPC) to maintain its highly efficient delivery system. Furthermore, it has reduced the number of carriers through its Core Carrier Concept. A four-module delivery system, purchased from Westinghouse, streamlines the process from the receipt of order through the choice of carriers. If a truck is only partially full, the system looks for other orders to complete the load. Then it selects the best carrier in terms of overall costs, service, equipment, and supply. First piloted at a central location in January 1997, the new system reduced Campbell's costs at that site by 16 percent. Now fully integrated throughout Campbell's, the system further cuts costs and makes shipping more efficient.

Development and Integration of Downstream Partnerships

Under Campbell's old distribution system, goods sometimes arrived in poor condition at customers' warehouses. Because shipping pallets were not standardized, the company had to take back damaged goods. To correct this problem, Campbell's contracted with a third-party rental company, Chep Pallets, to provide standardized pallets measuring 48 by 40 by 5 inches for all deliveries. The Chep Pallet program ensured more efficient arrangement of goods on trucks, reduced damage to goods, and increased the possible payload on each truck.

Evaluation and Streamlining: Direct Plant Shipping

To integrate its vast delivery system, logistics personnel from Campbell's meet regularly with logistics experts at customers' sites. Working with salespeople, these teams coordinate every step of the delivery process, from taking orders to issuing invoices.

In 1992, Campbell's began its Continuous Replenishment Program by which the company takes over the ordering process for its customers. Today, approximately 20 percent of Campbell's total volume is handled by continuous product replenishment, thereby avoiding delays, unnecessary paperwork, and damaged goods.

Moreover, its Direct Plant Shipping Program allows the company to reduce manufacturing costs by concentrating production of one or more items at a specific plant. Under normal conditions, products are shipped to a distribution center, then reloaded for shipment to customers. With Direct Plant Shipping, however, the company can offer its customers reduced costs if they buy directly from the manufacturing plant itself. Bypassing the distribution center and thus saving money, the company shares those savings with its customers, thereby improving its relationship with them.

Although most customers think of Campbell's as a company famous for its stable, traditional products, many are unaware of the vast changes that have occurred behind the scenes. The familiar red labels are still in place, but how those cans get to the shelves of the local supermarket is no longer simply a matter of trucks and purchase orders. Electronic commerce has streamlined Campbell's delivery chain, creating a seamless communication system with customers and assuring their satisfaction.

BEST-PRACTICE AGENDA

Become the "supplier of choice" by using out-of-box thinking to generate customer delivery solutions not bound by conventional wisdom, as New Pig Corporation, Norrell Corporation, and Holy Cross Hospital have done.

Customize delivery systems to fit the needs of core customers, in particular by creating channels of communication and service offerings to meet their demands. Establish a program similar to the CERRFS initiative undertaken by SARCOM.

Identify customer delivery requirements through a complete understanding of the impact that distribution has on a customer's business. As Granite Rock and Cemex show, often a best-practice company builds extensive lines of communication within its own system before streamlining its delivery services to customers.

Develop distribution capability as exemplified by Campbell's, paying close attention to small details—such as pallet size—that combine to solidify the customer-supplier relationship.

Top Ten Best-Practice Diagnostic Questions

1. How do you respond to customer delivery needs in emergency situations?

2. How do you identify the delivery service needs of individual customers? Do you use these needs as a method of customer segmentation?

3. Do you have just-in-time supply and continuous replenishment services?

4. What steps have you taken to ensure reliability in your delivery process? How do you communicate this process to your customers?

5. Do you have in-plant reps at customer sites? If so, what do you consider the biggest advantages of these relationships?

6. What is your delivery channel strategy? Do you align your delivery strategies to service specific customer needs?

7. Can you continuously track products from the production line to the customer's door?

8. Do you offer special delivery deals for large-scale purchases such as same-day shipping? Twenty-four-hour delivery? Any other customization features in packaging and delivery?

9. How do you differentiate your delivery strategy from competitors' in trying to become the supplier of choice?

10. What methods of feedback (other than a payment) do you get from customers regarding delivery and repair information? How do you elicit this input—via phone surveys, the Internet, or other means?

CHAPTER 7

TO SERVICE, WITH LOVE

How to Serve Your Customers Best

Subprocesses

Establish "Points-of-Contact" Excellence

Build Cross-Functional
"Points-of-Contact" Cooperation

Train Employees to Improve Customers'
Expectations for Products and Services

Best-Practice Companies

IBM

USAA

Coldwell Banker Relocation Services

Federal Express

Hyatt Hotels

The Disney Institute

East Jefferson General Hospital

The Walt Disney Company

Most companies would panic if their customer complaints shot up 500 percent. IBM, however, is ecstatic about such an increase.

In the good old days, many companies sang the old line "Don't bring me bad news." Confident that they were invulnerable, those companies chose not to listen to customer complaints, or if they did listen, they politely took down the information and promptly forgot it. Their mantra was *focus on the positive*. Even customer surveys were geared to elicit primarily favorable comments.

So why should Big Blue get ecstatic over customer complaints? Although IBM never stooped to such depths as completely disregarding customers, the company did, for a time, lose sight of just how important this asset is. "We stopped *listening* to our customers," says Ned Lautenbach, IBM's senior vice president of sales and distribution. "They talked to us and we sat there, but we really didn't respond."

Then in the early 1990s, IBM's stock fell to unprecedented levels, and stockholders demanded more than just an accent on the positive. In 1993, new CEO Louis Gerstner, Jr., took hold of the company in the midst of its restructuring, which included a new emphasis on providing customer service. As Lautenbach explains, "Probably the biggest thing Lou Gerstner did for our company was get us focused on our customers. He started by rebuilding a mind-set that says everything we do helps our customers compete more effectively and win in their marketplace. That's the foundation. Then we moved on to rework evaluation systems, compensation systems, and communications, all of which are essential to an organization dedicated to serving its customers."

A key element in developing stronger communications lies in knowing every response that an IBM customer has, the positive as well as the negative. As Lautenbach puts it, "We've found that we needed to hear more complaints to be able to understand what's on the customer's mind. Only then could we fix problems as our customers expected."

Now the company sings a new song in hopes that its customers will join in the chorus. And they do. Worldwide, IBM receives more than 50,000 customer complaints (excluding calls to the company's toll-free technical support system) each year. IBM customers receive surveys with ten specific questions on product quality and customer satisfaction. Teams of IBM employees from different areas across the company read surveys from those customers with whom they have previously dealt. Each team is empowered to take immediate action, if necessary, to solve a customer's complaint.

Each year IBM conducts some 40,000 customer interviews in 71 countries and in 26 languages. A central database catalogs the data and makes it available to a team of managers who generate company-wide initiatives. That database contains, according to Lautenbach, "every known problem that we've ever encountered, so we can go in, respond, and fix the customer's problem quickly. We set a goal in every country we do business in to be the best in our class in customer satisfaction. That's the case in more than half of the countries where we operate, twice as many as just three or four years ago."

As a major outgrowth of this new company attitude to customer service, IBM now allocates over twelve hundred employees from IBM Research to work with specific customers, often at the customer's site, on providing solutions such as creating algorithms for scheduling and ordering tickets. In addition, IBM has developed new technology that enables financial service companies to offer their clients better investment strategies such as online trading and risk-management systems. "IBM Research now devotes approximately 25 percent of its resources to funding this customer support," says Lautenbach. "It used to be zero percent or almost zero. So it's a dramatic change."

Another dramatic change is IBM's "Customer First" initiative. Begun in 1996, this program gives each frontline employee the authority without prior management approval to spend up to $5,000 *per incident* to solve problems for a customer on the spot. In its first year alone, these "point-of-contact" employees solved more than 600 customer incidents on the spot.

More complex problems call for the frontline employee to elicit the help of IBM executives. Managers from various regions in North America or from other countries constitute Customer Action Councils (CACs). Every council meets monthly to discuss with frontliners those issues that require extensive research, product development, or expenditures. As Jim Waugh, director of customer satisfaction for North America, describes them, the CACs offer senior management a way of saying to employees, "Bring us your problems, and we'll solve them together."

In addition, IBM's "Partnership Executive" program assigns 470 executives to more than 1,300 customer accounts, including many *Fortune* 500 companies and IBM's strategic business partners. These executives themselves function as "points of contact," much as their frontline counterparts. Each IBM executive in this program visits twice a year with client executives at each partner company to further strengthen customer relationships, which Lautenbach calls "the most valuable asset we have today at IBM."

As the central part of its restructure, providing excellence in customer service has enabled IBM to regain lost ground and reach new levels of success. The company has mastered this best practice by creating personalized, profitable relationships between employees and customers, and a strong sense of cooperation among its frontline and management staff, and establishing a training program that enables employees to better enhance the customer's experience with IBM products and services.

"Over the last four or five years," says Waugh, "what customers expect hasn't changed: They want an approachable company, knowledgeable follow-up, and basically a perfect encounter every time. That's impossible, of course, but we at IBM are getting closer." The following three subprocesses describe in greater detail just how close a best-practice company can get to perfection.

Subprocess 1
Establish "Points-of-Contact" Excellence

No one enjoys getting bounced around an automated telephone answering system, unable to contact a *real* human being who can answer a simple question or listen to a complaint. The same goes for computer systems that electronically record customers' opinions and release them into airless cyberspace. And no customer enjoys being transferred from department to department, receptionist to billing clerk, only to find that nobody knows the answer to the question of the moment. Companies that force their customers to break through organizational barriers to get issues resolved win few converts to their products and services.

Best-practice companies, however, realize the importance of establishing vital, one-on-one relationships with their customers at the earliest stage possible; indeed, like IBM and USAA (discussed below), they *aggressively pursue* customers for feedback, particularly if it is negative. The new business philosophy seems to be: "If you think it ain't broke, you probably haven't looked closely enough, and it's better to find out that the axle is cracked before you start out on a cross-country tour."

Customer-oriented companies establish "points of contact," employees whom customers know by name (if not by face) and whom they can call with any question or complaint, confident that their query will be taken seriously. Thoroughly trained to handle inquiries courteously and knowledgeably, company representatives or counselors often rely on computer technology to gather, sort, and direct customer complaints to the appropriate person or department. To build excellence in its points-of-contact program, best-practice companies update and expand this technology as their customer base grows or problems become more complex. Companies looking for ways to develop these systems often benchmark industry leaders such as IBM and USAA.

Finally, in order to establish points-of-contact excellence, a company should give its contact people the authority to make decisions and expedite customers' requests. Often this authority takes the form of a discretionary account that the employee can use to solve a problem on the spot. Ritz-Carlton Hotels, for example, authorizes employees to spend up to $2,000 per incident to make a guest more comfortable. The amount is less important than the act of creating the account, for the main point is for employees and customers to realize that the company values a speedy resolution to any problem and trusts its employees to provide point-of-contact excellence.

USAA may differ from other best-practice companies in that it has achieved point-of-contact excellence by investing heavily in computer technology. Still, its key to success in this area remains the same—keeping customer service personal and responsive.

USAA

Originally formed in 1922 by a group of U.S. Army officers, United States Automobile Association offered affordable auto insurance to military personnel and others who moved frequently from state to state. Today, USAA has almost 3 million members, including retired military personnel and their families, as well as 90 percent of all active-duty U.S. military officers. No longer in only the auto insurance business, USAA now provides extensive financial planning services, including consumer banking, life insurance, and investment products and services for such customer needs as mortgages, college tuition, and retirement. Although its insurance business is reserved for members, other products and services—such as the company's thirty-five mutual funds and investment services—are available to the general public. USAA, however, markets only to its specific niche; the general public "discovers" the company through word of mouth or mentions in the business press.

From its founding until the early 1990s, USAA—despite an increasing and increasingly successful use of technology to manage its various lines of business and make them more convenient for customers—did not have a formalized customer feedback system. The primary method of customer responses were customer letters to company executives and regular member surveys.

Then, in 1994, USAA designed, built, and installed its own computer technology that would capture any customer's query, complaint, or comment while that person was speaking to a USAA representative. (All the rep had to do was pull up a new screen, type in a short description of the problem, and send it to the appropriate area for action.) Called the ECHO system, an acronym for "Every Contact Has Opportunity," this system has transformed the way USAA provides customer service—and in a way that is invisible to the customer.

According to David Travers, executive director of USAA's service delivery and call center management, "ECHO has helped departments like mine get the noise level up on issues that affect the customer. In the past, if we changed the billing statement, for example, and customers didn't like the new format, it could take weeks or months before we got enough feedback to realize we had a problem. With ECHO, however, a change in billing might get seven hundred responses in three days, all telling us that we didn't get it right. With the new technology, it's like running a giant focus group all the time."

The USAA call center still receives input from customers by the traditional means (telephone, mail, and so forth), but now ECHO, as part of a separate department specializing in feedback management, not only allows customers to receive almost instant replies to their queries but also enables the company to mine the riches of those comments and change business processes accordingly.

The competitive advantage afforded by the ECHO system lies both in its capability of capturing information and responding in real time, and in its congruence with the team of knowledgeable, courteous representatives who maintain personalized contact with customers. USAA recognizes that technology without human contact is no solution to providing excellence in customer service. Other database systems give vital information necessary during a sales contact, for instance. If a customer calls seeking advice about an investment, and the USAA representative sees on his or her screen that this customer has a low tolerance for risk, the information gives the rep clear direction on how best to handle the inquiry.

USAA has plans to expand its point-of-contact excellence capabilities. As Karen Presley, senior vice president of marketing for USAA Capital Corporation, explains, "In the not too distant future, integrating a number of databases will allow us to start the next conversation with the customer exactly where we left off at the last call. With a complete, accurate picture of that member's relationship with USAA, we can better anticipate that customer's needs and provide the appropriate solution."

In the meantime, ECHO processes more than 2,000 customer calls each week, provides USAA management with an "early warning system" about industry trends and customer dissatisfaction, and improves how the company takes care of its customers. Over 86 percent of incoming calls are successfully handled during the first contact. Moreover, USAA has chalked up impressive statistics on customer satisfaction and retention: 73 percent of its clients are in the top quintile for customer satisfaction. Add in the second quintile, and the number jumps to 98 percent contented clients. As measured by renewal rates, customers' satisfaction with USAA auto insurance also tops the chart at 98 percent.

Based on these and other accomplishments in customer service excellence, a 1997 *Fortune* magazine survey ranked USAA 26 among 431 of America's most admired companies. Long known for its personalized relationships with its customers, USAA continues to point to its innovative use of technology to maintain customer support at a level that competitors only dream of reaching.

Subprocess 2
Build Cross-Functional "Points-of-Contact" Cooperation

Traditionally, customers have had to "do all the work" to get their problems solved. In many companies, the business units designed to serve the same customers rarely interact, and when they do, they seem at odds about how to handle problems or complaints.

To remedy this lack of agreement, companies today are looking for ways to improve cross-functional communication. Some assign customer accounts to teams of employees from various areas where contact with customers is paramount—for example, product design, marketing, sales, and accounts receivable. A single company contact might then have responsibility for all inquiries regarding credit, billing, collection, and, in some cases, even purchasing and order fulfillment.

Eliminating the layers of bureaucracy between customers and those employees best equipped to solve their problems is a first step in the subprocess of building cross-functional cooperation. As world-class companies have discovered, the best way to streamline customer service is to provide cross-functional training so that employees understand the entire customer cycle—from the first contact with a company to the follow-up that accompanies a sale and order fulfillment.

Next, companies need to establish bilateral communication between management and frontline employees. Some best-practice companies even require managers to take the jobs of frontliners for a day or assume a contributing role in a cross-functional team. Nothing isolates a manager like a closed office door, and best-practice companies such as IBM and The Walt Disney Company find ways to encourage managers to work side by side with others in the company (picking up trash in the theme park is part of Disney CEO Michael Eisner's job description).

This communication between managers and frontline employees, however, should be truly *bilateral.* Frontline employees should have the sense that management will listen seriously to any observations and suggestions they make. As IBM demonstrates, this subprocess can take place when a customer service representative brings to management's attention a serious problem that requires a heavy investment of capital and brain power to correct.

Finally, this subprocess usually relies on the development of a cross-functional database to identify any failure to provide adequate customer service. The best database will also collect those failures, categorize them, and provide analyses of when and why they occur. But however sophisticated the technology, the best practices in providing customer service ultimately come down to the people behind the machine—the managers who deal with customer problems in the abstract and the frontline representatives who deal with them daily on a face-to-face basis. Getting those two groups together—and giving them a chance to work cooperatively—is the essence of this subprocess.

COLDWELL BANKER RELOCATION SERVICES, INC.

After the death of a family member or a divorce, the relocation of a family from one house to another ranks as the third greatest producer of stress for human beings. No wonder, then, that employees who are being transferred by their companies constitute an emotional group of customers with a lot to do in very little time. These people need plenty of care, and counselors at Coldwell Banker Relocation Services (CBRS) empathize with their plight. CBRS representatives seize that opportunity to increase the attention they pay to customer service.

Recognizing that in the relocation industry there is no tangible product, Stephen Roney, president and CEO of CBRS, established an agenda of best practices and put the company's commitment to retain clients at the top of the list. In an industry that encounters people under some of life's most traumatic conditions, Coldwell Banker boldly guarantees its service fees to its customers.

As a testimony to the success of its strategy, the company boasts a 99 percent client retention rate. And most of those clients are price- and service-conscious companies that spend millions each year to relocate their employees. Coldwell Banker recognizes that customer service is not the province of one department or one group of people located down the hall on the third floor. Rather, customer service is *everyone's* responsibility.

In order to achieve such impressive numbers in client retention, the company has elevated cross-functional cooperation to the top of its list of corporate values. Specifically, it trains people throughout the organization to increase their understanding of the entire customer cycle; it has established strong bilateral communication between management and frontline employees; and it has created an effective means of understanding where and why failures in customer service occur. Once employees accept this system, they are more likely to be enthusiastic about undertaking the cross-functional training that will help them understand the entire customer cycle.

That cycle begins, of course, when a CBRS counselor first contacts a relocating family with information about services and products. Benchmarking the Lexus Company, CBRS management makes customer service its first order of business. Whether in a telephone conversation or at the first face-to-face meeting with a customer, the CBRS employee reviews the service evaluation tailor-made to that customer's particular needs and says: "These are the things that I need to perform well for you. If ever during our conversations or relationship I am not living up to being excellent in any of these areas, please let me know. It's my goal to serve you better than you've ever been served in a relocation process before."

As vice president for professional development, Denise Shields directs the company's training program with educational leaders in each regional office. Together this team plans a curriculum of courses ranging from "Behavioral Interviewing" to "Customer Service in the 90s" and invites staff members from throughout the company to attend. Although Coldwell Banker relocation counselors and account executives are typically the employees who have direct contact with customers, employees from other areas— resale management, acquisitions, and accounting, for example— are encouraged to undergo similar training because they will also provide services to the customer. CBRS accounting analysts, for example, process reimbursement checks to transferees for expenses associated with a move, and it is crucial to the customer's overall experience that those checks are issued accurately and promptly. Thus, accounting analysts undergo much of the same training that relocation counselors master.

In addition to formal cross-functional training of employees, Coldwell Banker has opened the lines of communication between senior management and frontline workers. Each year Leonard Troutner, executive vice president and COO, reads approximately 16,000 customer surveys, writes personal comments, and forwards the results to the relocation counselor or account executive who handled the customer's move. According to Shields, "Counselors feel as though senior management is involved in evaluating their accomplishments and recognizing their contributions." If a customer ever returns a negative evaluation, Troutner directs the response to the management team and instructs them to call immediately and find out why the customer was dissatisfied. Perhaps it is a one-time incident, but the evaluation can often point to a deeper problem that management must resolve.

CEO Roney also hosts three meetings each year with the company's national advisory board, which comprises nine representatives from CBRS's top clients. These meetings afford the management team an opportunity to discuss industry trends and new services as well as brainstorm about needs that CBRS clients will have in the immediate future—or five to ten years down the road.

CBRS management shares this information with everyone in

the organization, thereby providing not only a direct line of communication with frontline workers but also setting an agenda for regional and local meetings between CBRS personnel and their customers. Back on the local level, account executives conduct meetings on a regular basis with their customers and staff members, sharing information about program costs and the results of customer satisfaction surveys.

The company collects data from customer surveys and industry trends, feeds it into its database, and produces an extensive analysis of overall performance and customer satisfaction. This analysis does not get filed away on the shelf of a middle manager; the database turns out a trend analysis by client, counselor, and account executive for each regional office, then links that information directly to the company's employee incentive program. Once a month Coldwell Banker presents that data to the entire organization.

In undertaking this process, the company seeks to isolate specific points of failure, not point fingers at individual employees. If customers are unhappy, Coldwell Banker intends to do more than merely adjust service fees; it seeks to identify the root cause of the problem and then see that it does not occur again.

CBRS counts more than 500 corporate clients among its satisfied customers. In 1996, the company assisted almost 43,000 transferees through the arduous process of relocating homes and families, whether within a single city or from one continent to another. Its GlobalNet service provides a "local touch" to some 300 cities worldwide where CBRS counselors provide candidate assessment, policy briefings, international expense administration, and even cross-cultural training and immigration services. Clearly, in an industry where there is ample opportunity for things to go wrong, Coldwell Banker Relocation Services has earned its place among best-practice companies by building a strong customer service program.

In the process of designing a new database a few years back to focus more accurately on customers' needs, FedEx (previously profiled for its groundbreaking distribution methods in chapter 3) integrated two groups of employees that had traditionally been located on opposite ends of the creative spectrum: information technology experts and marketing representatives. Earlier, the "techies" drove the project by putting together the nuts and bolts of the system. Afterward, they helped get the marketing specialists up to speed. Once integrated, the groups were formed into teams that communicated on a regular basis and even engaged in joint off-site training.

The pairing was a huge success. Their combined efforts produced a database so effective that it elicited the same number of responses from 30 percent of the customers as the company's old system produced from surveys sent to 100 percent. In addition to providing FedEx with an immediate 70 percent cost savings in postage, the results showed that cross-functional communication could more effectively meet the customer's needs and increase productivity.

Now, whenever a new program is initiated at FedEx, marketing analysts and specialists form a team for the length of the project. By bringing their different skills and opinions together, the groups can better define the pulse of the public—and more powerfully deliver the company's products and services.

"At the end of the campaign we can go back and do an analysis of what worked with customers, what didn't work, and what was the shared learning," explains Sharanjit Singh, marketing director at FedEx. "The team can then figure out what to apply to the next program and also effectively share that learned information with all the other technical people and analysts within the company."

In addition to these employees, senior-level management and vice presidents also participate in the process, thus having everybody in the company with the same knowledge prior to dealing with customers. "The open communication between staff employees, directors, and managers at a professional level really makes for a lot of productive contrasts and opinions," Singh says. "Whenever there is a problem, it's addressed and talked about rather than left to fester. VPs from both the 'soft' side and the analytical side of marketing understand what we're trying to do and are there to lead, provide input, and support us."

Subprocess 3
Train Employees to Improve Customers' Expectations for Products and Services

If the database a company builds to record customer complaints (like the one at FedEx) can also analyze and direct inquiries to the person best equipped to answer them, this is certainly a step in the right direction. But to truly become a best-practice organization in providing customer service, the company first has to train its employees. They should be taught not only to make optimal use of the database but also to understand thoroughly the customer's experience with its product and services. As discussed in chapter 5, Lexus provides annual training for its salespeople, technicians, and customer service representatives to increase their appreciation of the customer's "Lexus experience"—from selecting options to driving away from the dealership the first time to the 100,000-mile checkup.

Best-practice companies such as The Walt Disney Company, East Jefferson General Hospital, and Hyatt Hotels begin their training with the recruiting process. They seek individuals who are strongly motivated to serve customers, who are good communicators, and who enthusiastically respond to the company's core values. Such companies offer continuous training through their own institutes, modeled after colleges and universities, with a curriculum of courses and seminars. Other best-practice companies use the team approach or mentoring to train employees, both new hires and veterans.

Underlying this subprocess is the principle that providing value-added information and services increases satisfaction and keeps customers loyal. Best-practice companies have learned that it is much less expensive to fix problems and preserve loyal customers than it is to go out and find new customers. Thus, the systematic capture of queries, requests, and complaints becomes an essential step in providing customer service excellence.

A final step in improving the customer's experience comes in acknowledging to the customer that the complaint has been heard and the problem fixed. It may cost no more than a first-class stamp and a personal letter, a phone call, or an E-mail to explain what the company has done to address the issue. On the other hand, a company such as IBM or USAA may allocate many weeks and dollars to solving the problem to customers' expectations.

HYATT HOTELS

At the Hyatt Regency Los Angeles, a couple had just finished breakfast and boarded a bus for the Los Angeles Convention Center where they were to be sworn in as new U.S. citizens. Suddenly they realized that they had made a terrible mistake: They had left their immigration papers folded up on a table at the hotel restaurant.

Rushing back to the Hyatt in a panic, they explained their plight to the restaurant manager, who relayed the story to three bussers. A few minutes later, waist-deep in garbage, one of the bussers held up the recovered documents like a trophy and handed them to the ecstatic couple, who hurried off to the swearing-in ceremony.

Such stories are not infrequent at Hyatt Hotels because the company systematically trains its employees to do whatever their guests need. The company even operates its own Hyatt University, where employees receive instruction in hospitality and hotel management as well as in the fundamental rules of human interaction (such as always making eye contact and greeting guests with a smile). The company's "Service Plus" training course takes up specific issues that guests have complained about and trains the employer on how to prevent these issues in the future.

In order to make this training more relevant, the company systematically captures queries, complaints, requests, and ideas that guests have made. Whether from phone calls, a hit on its Web site, or an individual survey, no response goes unnoticed or unrecorded. Indeed, in 1995, Hyatt began a random survey of approximately 800 guests annually at each of 98 hotels. Over the years since, it has constructed a database of some 140,000 responses that provide specific details of failures in customer service. To ensure that those complaints do not recur, guest comments are faxed directly to the general manager at the individual hotels. Each month a cross-functional team led by Hyatt's senior vice president of operations takes up a critical issue culled from guest feedback and develops a best practice to address critical guest concerns, issues, and insights. Every hotel in the Hyatt system receives a copy of each best practice that this team generates for distribution throughout the hotel.

Customers need to have the sense that their complaints and suggestions are heard and acted on, not just tossed into a trash bin. Best-practice companies, therefore, look for ways to shorten the response time between receiving a complaint and doing something about it. And among best-practice companies, Hyatt stands out for its extraordinarily short response time. One business customer, for example, checked into the Denver Hyatt but in his haste had forgotten to make the necessary reservation for the room he wanted. Upon entering the room he was given, he turned on the television and was greeted by a screen with the Hyatt customer survey. Using the TV's remote control, he punched in his evaluations and thought nothing more about the survey. To his surprise and delight, however, within *five minutes* of receiving the electronic communication, the hotel manager called him to say that although the hotel was entirely booked and the room could not be changed, the guest could expect a hospitality gift for his inconvenience. The business executive was suitably pleased with the gift but completely flabbergasted by the rapid response time. If only he could get his own people to respond that fast!

As a best-practice company that thoroughly trains its employees to enhance the customer's experience, Hyatt has learned the value of real-time tracking of customer complaints and queries. Just as some companies monitor the cost of running a machine or operating a manufacturing process, Hyatt believes there is equal value in tracking a customer's response to the hotel's service. "We believe in person-to-person, hotel-to-guest resolution," says John Romano, Hyatt's director of quality assurance. "We have a lot of faith in our general managers, who are responsible for multimillion-dollar properties. They understand the importance of service recovery, and they've taken it to heart."

By systematically following up on each customer survey, those managers have alerted their employees to problems demanding resolution. Whether it is a vending machine on one hotel's sixth floor that eats quarters or a more general issue such as the smell of freshness that greets a guest upon first entering a room, Hyatt is prepared to channel service requests to thoroughly trained personnel who can get the job done.

THE DISNEY INSTITUTE

Walt Disney's own philosophy on business was simple: "Give the public everything you can give them. Keep the place as clean as you can, keep it friendly, and make it a fun place to be." After completing his first theme park, Disneyland, in 1955, Walt began developing a training concept to complement this thinking. The result was Disney University, which heralded itself as the world's first *corporate* university.

Initially comprising a global network of training centers for Disney's own employees, Disney U. began in 1986 to offer programs for other companies to learn business Magic Kingdom-style inside the Walt Disney World theme park. Now officially known as the professional development arm of Disney Institute, a 57-acre campus on park grounds that also offers personal enrichment programs for vacationers and a youth component, it instills Walt's belief that "where you learn is as important as what you learn." The institute turns the park itself into a living classroom. The development programs give companies of all sizes—from *Fortune* 500 members such as IBM and Westinghouse to small, single-locale businesses—the opportunity to engage in two diverse types of learning. Business and management programs focus on the time-tested techniques for service, personnel management, and creativity that make Disney a best-practice company; in contrast, behind-the-scenes tours bring students "backstage" for a peek into the methods and functions behind Disney magic.

Using the business and management component, a company's supervisors, executives, and frontline employees can all learn to adapt a variety of Disney's business methods into their own systems. The four-day "Customer Loyalty: Keeping the Promise" program, for instance, offers strategies on how to retain long-term customers by developing an infrastructure of processes and practices to earn the loyalty of employees and customers; increasing market share and revenues while decreasing the cost to acquire and service customers; and building individual relationships with customers. Shorter, three-hour workshops provide insights into the Disney approach through group discussions, activities, and take-home workbooks, whereas one-day sessions include classroom participation and a guided field experience to scrutinize park activities.

In behind-the-scenes tours like "Innovation and Action," groups go to such areas as the Disney rehearsal facilities, waste water treatment plant, tree farm, and the "Utilidor," a network of tunnels beneath the Magic Kingdom park. With excursions to the "Casting Center," where Disney uses its innovative hiring techniques to find new employee "cast members," these programs focus on the cutting edge of creativity and design. At Epcot, groups explore the unique architectural styles and systems of an experimental environment, while planting and environmental tours shed light on conservation and recycling practices as well as the changing shape of Disney's horticulture.

Disney's "customizing teams" conduct a needs analysis evaluation and develop a training program tailored to the individual client. Groups ranging from five to five thousand attend Disney's business and management seminars, receive a behind-the-scenes tour, or work with Disney Institute personnel to gear sessions to fit into the visiting company's presentation.

"You can dream, create, design, and build the most beautiful place in the world," Walt Disney said shortly before his death, "but it requires people to make it a reality." As companies such as East Jefferson General Hospital have found, the practices that make

The Walt Disney Company a best-practice company can work just as well for businesses whose primary product is not make-believe.

EAST JEFFERSON GENERAL HOSPITAL

Companies in the health care industry make up the largest percentage of any field among the corporate visitors to training programs at Disney Institute. One longtime regular on campus has been East Jefferson General Hospital of Metairie, Louisiana. Managers from East Jefferson General made their first trip to the Disney Institute in 1990, hoping to come away with methods for making their employees more cognizant of patient and family needs. The hospital's CEO, Peter Betts, had already enacted sensitivity training and other internal efforts with some success but felt these programs were going stale. A fresh approach was needed, and he got it.

"I was overwhelmed," Betts recalls of his first look at the Disney program. "There were several major messages I came away with. One was Disney's emphasis that employees become cast members: When they put on their uniforms or costumes, their whole attitude changes. They wear a different face when interacting with the public, and they do everything with the customer in mind. Perhaps most impressive to me was the way they had made understanding their customers' expectations the top priority."

Betts took the lessons back to Metairie and looked again at the environment inside East Jefferson General. He looked at things from a different angle—the patients' point of view. By observing how patients and visitors moved about the hospital, he realized that many appeared confused—and for good reason: The hospital had outgrown its old system for helping people find their way.

He brought in focus groups to offer their opinions. Physically challenged patients, for instance, told him that many water fountains and bathrooms at the hospital were inaccessible. Taking his Disney training to heart, Betts expanded the hospital's patient satisfaction survey: All patients now receive a questionnaire seeking their opinions on different areas of service. Feedback from these surveys and every other patient contact are routed among the entire East Jefferson General staff.

"We saw people wandering around looking for the radiology department, so we tore down all our signs and redid them," explains Betts. "We had wheelchair or handicapped-accessible bathrooms only in our rehab units, which is pretty dumb when you think about it, so we took care of that. We asked people everything—starting with their impressions when they first walked into the hospital—and then followed up on them. The practice was so successful that now we do whatever we can to get that customer-oriented point of view."

Focus groups remain an ongoing feature at East Jefferson General. Combinations of current patients, former patients, and community members regularly offer input on a variety of issues. In an effort to track complaints and requests, hospital staff—now called "team members"—join the sessions and spread word of whatever new views they pick up among their teammates. Like cast members at the Magic Kingdom, they are eager to put fresh ideas into action and meet customer needs.

The East Jefferson General management team has put several elements in place to make sure every member of the staff is ever-ready to improve the experience of patients, family members, and other guests. In the nursing unit, for example, workers coach new team members until they can confidently meet standards. When members of the food and nutrition staff take on a new role, a well-versed team member "shadows" them to observe their interactions with patients and provides suggestions for improvement.

When warranted, the staff revises the customer satisfaction

survey to include those questions that individual patients have recently asked. For example, when patients found the billing system difficult to understand, the hospital made it more succinct and thereby cut customer calls in half. When patients commented on the personal appearance of staff members, the hospital established for its employees the "EJ Look," basic expectations for grooming and dress based on patient expectations and staff input.

One year many patients requested shorter wait times, so the hospital formed a process improvement team to study how team members could better meet customer time constraints. "Wait time in the emergency department could be attributed to waiting for the ED physician, waiting for the specialist, waiting for X-ray or lab work, or any number of other things," explains Betts. "Now we cross-train emergency department people, for instance, to do the lab work. Such innovations save turnaround time and cut down on the time patients have to wait."

From the moment new team members join the East Jefferson General Hospital staff, they are constantly evaluated on how they provide value-added services to customers and fellow team members. "One-half of each merit system raise is based on customer service," says Betts. "You can be the best technical person in the world, but if you don't meet the minimum grade in guest relations, you don't get a raise. Most doctors are not trained in patient sensitivity. Since we're starting our own family medicine residency program [in July 1998], we're going to teach our resident physicians the importance of guest relations."

As a result of all these efforts, patients with even the most specialized needs can get them met at East Jefferson General. One couple arrived at the hospital, the wife in labor and the husband having a heart attack. The husband wanted to be with his wife, so the cardiologist personally pushed the husband's bed from the coronary care unit onto an elevator and down to the wife's room.

The bed wouldn't fit through the doorway, so the cardiologist sat in the hallway with the husband until 3:00 A.M. so he could talk to his wife through the door until it was time for her delivery.

On its own initiative, the hospital's clerical staff began mentoring new secretaries. This practice has since spread into a hospital-wide buddy system. Now, whether ordering stethoscopes, admitting visitors, or bathing a patient, every team member at East Jefferson General has at least one other person to offer suggestions on how to improve delivery of value-added customer services.

This same approach has even impacted new construction at the hospital. Patients used to complain that they got lost or tired trekking from East Jefferson General's parking garages to various hospital departments. When the Domino Healthcare Pavilion outpatient facility was being planned, many Disney concepts were incorporated in the design and systems prior to its summer 1997 opening. The area that connects the garage to the main building was designed to allow patients to park on floors linked to specific departments. By parking on the "Outpatient Surgery" level, for instance, a patient can now walk across the garage and directly into that department.

"It's thirty-five steps from the vestibule located on every garage floor to the first point of service," says Betts. "Each vestibule is manned by one of our red-jacketed guest relations representatives, who helps you out of your car and assists you to where you need to go."

The "red jackets" are another way that East Jefferson General enhances a visitor's experience. As part of the improvements made to help visitors and patients reach their destination, guest relations representatives were placed just inside the hospital's front doors. Part of the impetus for this idea came from Betts's visit to the Orlando Hyatt, where crimson-clad bellhops exemplify excellence in customer service.

East Jefferson General's red jackets are getting plenty of work. There were nearly 225,000 outpatient visits to the hospital in 1996 alone, and *every* patient still received a questionnaire upon leaving. The hospital has established what it considers an acceptable "overall hospital guest relation score" and measures customer satisfaction with various departments such as nursing, radiology, and food services. Staff members in each department discuss their scores, and any questionnaire that identifies a service problem or general patient unhappiness is forwarded to the administrative director or line officer responsible for the department cited.

"Every complaint gets a personal phone call or follow-up letter," says Betts, who answers his own mail and makes such calls himself. "We're actually pleased when we get negative comments because it gives us an opportunity to identify a problem and put something in place to keep it from happening again."

Further value-added services for patients and the community surrounding East Jefferson General include a "Speakers Bureau" offering free seminars, in which hospital team members discuss everything from medication management to cancer prevention. These seminars attract more than 10,000 people a year and include speakers chosen from a database of doctors, nurses, dietitians, and other health care professionals. In the "Elder Advantage" program, nearly 45,000 members age fifty and over can attend programs on the East Jefferson General campus geared to them.

Just how successful has East Jefferson General Hospital been in benchmarking the best practices of Disney? In 1997, the Disney Institute awarded the hospital with a "Mouscar"—a statuette of Mickey Mouse (their version of the Oscar)—for being the company that best exemplifies the Disney methods of delivering customer service. This is the first time Disney has given such recognition to another organization. The positive response generated from East Jefferson General's internal changes and the Mouscar (presented to Betts by Mickey himself) have helped boost the hospital's popularity to the point where some 10,000 applicants seek to be among the 400 hired annually. Turnover among current team members has dropped from 18 percent in 1990 to 11.2 percent—less than half the industry average of 25 percent.

Although it competes with five other hospitals in the same area, 57 percent of those people polled in its primary service area said East Jefferson General was their hospital of choice for general health care needs (its highest-ranked competitor received only 19 percent). The numbers are similar for emergency services, inpatient admissions, and several other parameters. Since East Jefferson General began using patient testimonials ten years ago, it has accumulated a waiting list of people willing to sing the hospital's praises in collateral materials and ads. One woman felt compelled to go to the hospital on her own time and spend fifteen minutes gushing in a management team meeting about the excellent care she had received. Over a hundred other hospitals in the United States and Canada have taken tours through East Jefferson General to see the magic for themselves. In addition, viewing the videotape footage of the Mouscar-winning team in action has now become a regular part of the training at the Disney Institute in Orlando.

"Because of the way the managed care provider networks are set up, there is no financial incentive for a patient to come to our hospital instead of our competitors," says Betts. "So I think patients' perceptions of quality are a big factor in the choice of where to go. How are they treated? Does a nurse come when they press the call button? When someone enters their room, does that person knock first? What happens when patients call with complaints?

Whatever we can do to improve their experience, we're going to do it."

THE WALT DISNEY COMPANY

Among the principles that have made The Walt Disney Company one that East Jefferson General Hospital and hundreds of other organizations benchmark is the value Mickey and Company place on personalizing customer service. Points-of-contact excellence are referred to as "magic moments," and as displayed by such examples as Mickey's Starland and character breakfasts (described in chapter 4), the company will go to great lengths to attain them. Disney's carefully screened employee "cast members" are taught to make each interaction with an individual customer an incident of lasting impression. Each employee strives for 60 such exchanges in the course of one eight-hour shift. With some 45,000 cast members at its Florida resort alone, Disney management gives guests plenty of enchantment for their money.

Management realizes that most people seeking jobs at Walt Disney World or one of the other theme parks have themselves been Disney guests in the past; accordingly, prospective employees, as well as old-timers, have clear expectations about what the Disney "experience" means to visitors. Disney promises not only a fantasy visit to Cinderella Castle and a trip to Tomorrowland but also clean streets, friendly faces, and never a disgruntled employee. To create this atmosphere, Disney goes to extraordinary lengths to recruit and train employees, following a rigorous process to ensure that customers have the time of their lives.

Although the company wants its employees to be enthusiastic, it also wants them to know that jobs within the Magic Kingdom are not all fun. As Disney's former manager of customer satisfaction, Valerie Oberle, explains, "When it's ninety-five degrees out and ninety-five percent humidity and you get asked 'Where are the bathrooms?' for the three-hundreth time that day while you're working a popcorn wagon—which I have done—that's not all pixie dust and glamour. It's hard work. So we have to manage the reality of what it's like to work here with their expectations of coming to work for a fantasy organization."

To become a Disney employee, each person has to begin thinking of himself or herself as a member of a team—actually a cast member. Even though many do not appear on a literal stage, still the show must go on.

First, Disney human resource managers conduct thorough interviews of prospective employees. "For the majority of our forty-five thousand cast members—most of whom are entry-level service workers—it's really more of an internal check, kind of a look into their hearts," says Oberle. "Do they really care about people? Do they have high standards for themselves? What are their personal values? Do they like good hard work, whether at eight A.M. or midnight?"

Before even filling out an application, each Disney prospect is ushered into a building called "Central Casting." Turning a handle resembling the Doorknob character from *Alice in Wonderland,* they enter a long hallway lined with statuettes and paintings of Disney characters. Next they watch a ten-minute video, a lighthearted film with a serious message that informs them about the tough schedule (open 365 days a year), strict guidelines for employees' appearance, and the need to provide their own transportation. After viewing this movie, approximately 20 percent decide against seeking Disney jobs. "It's a fabulous way for us to treat potential cast members as guests, make them feel good about the process, and allow them to screen themselves out," says Oberle. "It's an efficient way for us to manage our business."

Once hired, new employees join their fellow cast members, including everyone from top management to monorail operators. Each plays a role in the show, explains Oberle, and training starts the same for every new hire. At a two-day initiation process known as "Disney Traditions," vice presidents, housekeepers, and popcorn poppers are enrolled together in classes of forty at the Disney Institute. The company pays no attention to rank. The students wear tags with only first names because in this environment everyone is on a first-name basis. The only people afforded special status are guests.

"We start with talking about the big picture, what The Walt Disney Company is," says Oberle. "It's overwhelming to work here. Walt Disney World is a huge place, with a zillion guests a year. We want our people to be as connected as possible and feel as comfortable as possible."

Whether one works "backstage" or "onstage," the focus is always on the "quality show." Split into smaller groups, the rookies go into the Magic Kingdom to observe veteran workers as they interact with guests. Occasionally, a veteran turns to a rookie and asks how he or she might handle a particularly difficult encounter. "We set the stage and build the culture," says Oberle.

During this process, new hires learn Disney's four cardinal principles of guest relations—safety, courtesy, show, and efficiency—which together provide a framework for all decisions made in the facility's operating areas. Devised by Walt Disney himself, this sequencing is purposeful: A customer's safety should always come first, at the sacrifice of everything else—including a good show. Guests expect courtesy, and cast members learn to be patient and friendly even when sweating it out in a Donald Duck costume.

Everything a guest can hear, touch, smell, or feel should be considered part of the "show": clean streets, piano music, the smell of popcorn, great skits with fantastic dancing and special effects.

It's the same thing with efficiency: If monorails don't run on time, guests have to wait in long lines; if computers at the hotel check-in line go down, the show falters.

To display the logic of these principles in action, Oberle uses the example of the continuous-motion walkways located at the start of several rides. In order for elderly people, those with trouble walking, and guests in wheelchairs to enjoy such attractions, cast members running them will stop the walkways momentarily to allow these guests to get on and move to their seats. The "show" element of the ride is briefly sacrificed, and customer safety is put first. The cast member at the Haunted Mansion attraction, for example, might make an excuse for stopping the ride, using an explanation that becomes part of the show: "Playful spooks have interrupted our tour. Kindly remain seated in your Doom Buggy, please. We will begin our tour momentarily." This instruction is in line with the overall success formula at Disney, the combination of a quality guest experience, quality cast member experience, and quality business practices.

After the two-day initiation, new hires begin to connect with their specific work locations. They meet their supervisors as well as their Disney Qualified Trainer, a veteran at the same job always available to answer questions. With an outline and checklist, new employees start training programs of varying lengths. Human resources managers at each facility monitor new cast members to make sure the process runs smoothly.

"Training" is not reserved just for new hires, however. Even longtime Disney employees have to relearn their roles in order to give customers the best show. The grounds at every theme park are world famous for their spotlessness—a reputation to which every Disney employee contributes. Garbage cans are strategically placed no farther than twenty-five feet apart throughout the facility, and all employees have trash collection as part of their job descriptions. They don't have to worry about strewn newspapers; no papers or magazines are sold inside the facility, so guests can truly forget the outside world and get caught up in the magic.

One of the expressions that has become part of the company culture in recent years is "bump the lamp." It refers to a scene in the animated Disney film *Roger Rabbit* in which a character bumps into a lamp and causes it to shake briefly. Close observation shows that the shadow of the lamp also shakes, a detail only the most scrutinizing of moviegoers would notice. CEO Michael Eisner has since set the goal for all his employees to "bump the lamp" whenever possible—to push for a higher level of quality that, even if unnoticed by most guests, aims at perfection and evokes pride in the entire cast.

New employees are taught to look at the emotions, needs, and expectations of guests at each part of their visit. Guests entering the park in the morning are usually in a cheerful, upbeat mood, so cast members working the front ticket windows should be talkative and friendly—asking folks where they're from and paying special attention to children. Employees handling the gate at day's end, however, are instructed to treat guests very differently: Visitors leaving the park are often tired, and they want nothing more than a quiet good-bye and directions to the nearest monorail or parking lot. Cast members—many of whom are aspiring actors and actresses—seem to enjoy the chance to actually "perform" as part of their jobs.

Even after guests have left for the parking lot, the focus on customer service continues. Perhaps due to their excitement upon reaching the park, 20,000 Disney guests lock their keys in their car each year. To combat this problem, cast members roam the parking lots offering assistance with free keymaking and other services. When guests forget where they parked their car, they need only tell an attendant approximately when they arrived at the park to get the issue resolved. The lots are filled one at a time each morning on the same time schedule, so "if you came at ten A.M., you must be in Goofy Lot C."

"The heart and soul of the whole issue to get to a high level of quality service is to *take care of your people*," says Oberle. "Whether they're directly delivering a service or they're backstage boxing it up or folding it, they're doing something to get it ready to deliver to the customer."

Oberle gives the following formula for Disney's success in training employees to meet customers' expectations: "Recruit the right people, train them, continually communicate with them, ask their opinion, involve them, recognize them, and celebrate with them. If you show respect for their opinions and you involve them, they will be proud of what they do—and they will deliver quality service to your guests."

BEST-PRACTICE AGENDA

Establish primary "points of contact" between your employees and customers, instilling in customers the feeling that their needs are being met personally and promptly. By using the company's computer-based ECHO system, USAA reps can individually record and respond almost immediately to client queries and problems. At the same time, the information can be used to alter company-wide business processes.

Build cross-functional cooperation by training employees to understand and enhance the entire customer experience, then holding them responsible for customer satisfaction. This training could come via improving lines of communication between management and frontline employees—much as Coldwell Banker Relocation Services does—or by instructing employees how to treat customers from the first point of contact, such as Hyatt and Disney.

Create a database to identify customer service failures and embrace their identification, recalling the principle that drives customer satisfaction at IBM and FedEx: Your customers know best what they don't like and what they can't understand.

Raise customer expectations for products and services by giving them high-quality treatment each step of the way. Whether it is greeting guests at the front door, as the Red Jackets do at East Jefferson General Hospital, or helping guests locate keys to their locked cars, as Disney World attendants do, the best-practice company personalizes its customer service at every point of contact.

Make sure each employee has at hand all information needed to process a customer's request promptly and efficiently. Providing this information may require sophisticated databases such as those used by Hyatt Hotels to identify specific guests' needs and FedEx has in place to help customers track shipments. Or the organization may assemble data from customer surveys and distribute it as needed to appropriate personnel, much as East Jefferson General Hospital has done by collecting information from groups such as senior citizens to better prepare employees associated with its Elder Advantage program.

Top Ten Best-Practice Diagnostic Questions

1. What is your customer retention rate? Does it indicate any trends you can act upon?

2. What is the level of cross-functional communication between your company and its customers?

3. Do you train employees throughout the organization in various tasks so that any of them can handle any problem that arises during the customer cycle?

4. What financial empowerment do you provide to your front-

line employees to solve customer problems? Do you give them additional authority to make decisions on the spot?

5. Do those frontline employees have access to executive groups such as IBM's customer action councils where they can receive additional assistance and powers of authority?

6. Do you have in place a cross-functional database to track and analyze customer service highlights and lowlights?

7. How do you explicitly gauge your customers' satisfaction? Do focus groups play a role?

8. Is any portion of your company's merit system based on customer service?

9. Do you have a client advisory board? How often does it meet? What does it accomplish?

10. Do you surprise your customers with great customer service as East Jefferson General Hospital does with its red-jacketed representatives who accompany visitors to their destinations?

CHAPTER 8

MINDING THE STORE OF DATA

How to Manage Customer Information

SUBPROCESSES

BUILD CUSTOMER PROFILES
ESTABLISH SERVICE INFORMATION
MEASURE CUSTOMER PERFORMANCE AND SATISFACTION

BEST-PRACTICE COMPANIES

AMERICAN EXPRESS
RITZ-CARLTON HOTELS
BLACK & DECKER
PEAPOD
ORANGE COUNTY TEACHERS FEDERAL CREDIT UNION

Buy anything these days—a new automobile, a pair of shoes, a collar for the family pet—and chances are that someone somewhere will record that purchase in a database and prepare a marketing package for the next morning's mail. Savvy companies such as Lexus, Peapod, and Fingerhut know not only what their customers prefer but also when they are likely to make their *next* purchase, how much they are willing to spend, and even where they will buy a product or service. Marketing, in other words, has gone high-tech.

Leading the charge is American Express, the financial services company with global reach, not to mention the world's largest travel agency and American Express Financial Advisors, a one-hundred-year-old financial planning company, as well as American Express Financial Direct, an online brokerage service. Although highly diversified, American Express never loses sight of its 41.5 million cardmembers, some 27 million in the United States alone, and those are just the individuals who never leave home without their American Express or Optima card. Add to that number the thousands of merchants with whom American Express partners, and the actual number of customers is much greater.

Keeping track of all those customers could become a logistics nightmare, but as we have seen in chapter 3, American Express has managed to turn customer data into a sustainable competitive advantage. The company does so by *managing customer information*, a process that proceeds according to the following three steps:

1. Build customer profiles to identify purchasing patterns, attitudes, and values.

2. Establish service information to discover how and when customers actually use the company's products and services.

3. Measure customer performance and satisfaction to determine which aspects of a product or service customers value most. These performance measures include pricing, expedient and accurate customer service and billing, and an array of optional features. Feedback from customers enables a company to measure its success in satisfying their needs and wants.

To service cardmembers and merchant relationships, American Express maintains information about cardmembers' spending with each merchant, who is also an American Express customer. As mentioned in chapter 3, if a customer uses the American Express card to charge a pair of shoes at a particular store, that information can be shared with the store's owner, who on his own might not be able to keep track of customers' purchases and preferences. Working with American Express, which provides information from its vast database, that merchant can offer special discounts to his or her best customers. For example, the customer's next monthly statement could include an offer such as "Buy another pair of shoes at this store and receive 25 percent off."

By further managing its relationships between customers and merchants, American Express can leverage its "closed loop" network to create added value for both customers and merchants while building loyalty on both sides. Through the company's Custom Extras program, representatives analyze the data in order to customize rewards for individual cardholders based on purchasing history. According to Amy Radin, American Express vice president of rewards development, the company's chief competitors—the major bank credit cards—"don't have as detailed cardmember data or merchant data. American Express owns both of those relationships in their entirety, so that gives the company a huge competitive advantage."

Merchants like the program because it enables them to reach and keep loyal customers they might otherwise lose. Acting on their own, merchants would incur significantly higher expenses to build their own loyalty programs with customers. Cardmembers like the program because, often when they least expect a bonus, they are rewarded for shopping at stores they prefer. And American Express likes the program because it appeals to millions of customers, no matter where they concentrate their spending. Frequent flier programs offered by most major airlines on travel, retail purchases, or entertainment, on the other hand, can reach only a limited audience.

American Express analyzes cardmember data to define the types of offers that will be most relevant and valuable for its customers. After creating profiles of best customers, marketing representatives analyze the information to determine how best to reward those customers. "Express Rewards," a program begun in early 1997, tells merchants at the point of sale that the purchaser is a VIP customer who has satisfied certain criteria predetermined by the merchant. For example, a customer checks into a hotel and guarantees the room with an American Express card. The merchant instantaneously receives verification that this is an Express Rewards customer—a "VIP" symbol flashes on the computer screen at the reservations desk—and the hotel can surprise the guest with an upgrade, knowing that he or she has visited the hotel three times earlier during a specified period.

Another special offers program comes from American Express Travel Services. Knowing that some of its customers frequently use the Internet to search for cheap flights, the company offers last-minute travel bargains online. Because of the added value they bring, not to mention the surprise factor, such American Express programs help build long-term customer loyalty.

Furthermore, American Express recognizes that customer satisfaction hinges on more than just a good product. Today's increasingly discriminating customers want a variety of easy-to-use products to choose from, quick delivery, and higher levels of dependability and service. Upon discovering that customers are not using its products and services to their best advantage, a company can engage in educational programs to help them get the most out of those products and services, thereby increasing satisfaction levels. American Express Small Business Services, for instance, sends a monthly statement to each business owner detailing every charge that individual employees have made to the company's account. This statement allows the owner to determine who is spending what and to manage expenses more appropriately.

According to Amy Radin, American Express "takes feedback from customers very seriously. We read how cardmembers view our products versus the competition's. We're much more interested in how the cardmembers perceive the competition than our own views of it."

Sharing the information contained in its database throughout the company, American Express improves services and customer satisfaction. The American Express billing statement now contains targeted marketing promotions to help specific customers take advantage of offers made by partnering merchants of American Express.

In short, American Express measures customer satisfaction through its extensive database, by which it collects cross-functional information about customers' use of products and services. The company surveys customers to determine the key drivers for using American Express's credit services rather than a competitor's. Those factors include customers' desire for value, service quality, dependability, accurate billing, and special rewards for loyalty. By knowing these preferences and tracking other customer information, American Express takes steps to ensure its current and future success.

Subprocess 1
Build Customer Profiles

Not all customers are created equal, nor do they behave or look the same. And what they need on Monday may differ markedly from what they request on Thursday. Accordingly, a customer database helps a company determine what products suit what customers and where profitability lies. For instance, a company can use this information to distinguish those valuable customers on whom it should focus its most costly retention efforts from those marginal customers who may not require such an expensive approach. As American Express has learned, customer databases provide a useful tool for leveraging information to develop specific marketing offers.

When they hear the term *customer database,* many managers think first of costly technology and time-consuming data processing. Database marketing, however, has many levels of complexity. A PC and software may be all that many small- or medium-size companies need to create customer profiles. This level of technology can easily store and process information about patterns in customers' purchasing, direct marketing campaigns, and degree of customer loyalty. Larger companies can use more complex technology for mining information to unearth hidden patterns of customer behaviors. As discussed below, Ritz-Carlton Hotels can identify customers' preferences and alert every hotel in its chain to them within minutes.

RITZ-CARLTON HOTELS

A host attempting to impress party guests is often said to be "putting on the Ritz," whereas someone trying to downplay a less-than-glamorous spread may offer the excuse, "It's not the Ritz, but it's the best I could do." In both cases the comments are a way of comparing current standards to those exemplified by one of the world's most respected and benchmarked companies.

The name Ritz-Carlton has become synonymous with all things elegant. At the same time, the hotel chain has developed a reputation for stellar customer service, earning it a Malcolm Baldrige National Quality Award in 1992—the first hospitality organization ever to receive the honor. Two years later, the Ritz-Carlton strategy of using information systems to better serve customers was first taught at Harvard Business School. According to a study done by an independent research company, approximately 95 percent of Ritz-Carlton guests leave with the impression that they have had a "memorable visit."

The company's philosophy is perhaps best summed up in its credo: "The Ritz-Carlton experience enlivens the senses, instills well-being, and fulfills even the unexpected wishes and needs of our guests." Much of the secret behind the ability of Ritz-Carlton employees to live up to these words lies in the company's competence in tracking and fulfilling customers' needs. Each Ritz-Carlton staff includes one or two guest recognition coordinators whose main task is to research the preferences of every guest at their hotel. The coordinators receive a list of all incoming guests, then link these names to a guest-history database that tells them every previously recorded incident between the guest and the Ritz-Carlton chain. Since the database was established in 1992, it has grown to contain histories and preferences of over a half million guests. Over that same span, guest retention has improved by 25 percent.

"The guest recognition coordinators go to the executive committee meeting at their hotel every morning," explains Allison Frantz, corporate manager of training and development for Ritz-Carlton. "There they can tell the general manager, rooms division manager, food and beverage manager, and everyone else about the VIPs and other guests who may have had previous difficulties coming in that day, as well as any other information on new high-profile guests. Maybe somebody likes chocolate or enjoys having dinner early. This is the time to pass that information along so we can be ready with a box of candy or early dinner time when the guests check in."

The Ritz-Carlton compiles customer profiles in part through observations made by hotel staff in the course of their normal duties. Each staff member carries a guest preference pad on which to record any notes that may lead to enhanced customer service down the road. If housekeepers enter a room and see a tennis racket, tennis shoes, and tennis magazines, they might write down that "Mr. Smith in Room 312 seems to enjoy tennis." They then convey their observation to coordinators, who alert appropriate staff members to contact the guest with available court times and other services beginning that day. The coordinator also places this information in the database, so the next time the guest checks into any Ritz-Carlton, the staff will be ready and waiting with the same services. The morning paper, a nonallergenic pillow, a glass of orange juice at 6:00 A.M.—all will be there without the need to ask.

A similar system is used to handle what Frantz calls "difficult guest encounters." If a guest shows displeasure or anger over a particular incident or service, the employee involved fills out a form detailing the incident, the reasons for the guest's dissatisfaction, and the employee's attempt to rectify the situation. (Employees are empowered to spend up to $2,000 without prior approval to resolve a customer problem.) This information also goes into the database, where it is shared with various hotel departments, all but ensuring that the same mistake does not happen again.

"If the guest had a bad experience with room service in Atlanta, for instance, the coordinators in Kansas City will read about it when the guest is checking in there," says Frantz. "They can call Atlanta to get more details on the situation, then instruct their staff to be more sensitive to the needs of that guest."

Cross-functional training is another way the Ritz-Carlton guarantees that its guests will have "every need fulfilled." The company offers its employees a self-directed work team environment along with classes in ten different areas, ranging from payroll management to scheduling to peer review training. Although employees receive a pay increase for each class they complete, the benefit to customers, according to Frantz, is worth far more than the cost of raising salaries. "Managers now have more of their time free to get involved in more visionary things like process and product management as well as coaching, counseling, and development," she says, "and workers who understand and share each other's responsibilities learn to work much more cohesively as a team to meet customer needs."

Subprocess 2
Establish Service Information

Stories abound about the strange uses that customers devise for products. There's the old story about a woman who ordered a Sears catalog and then promptly put it to use as a doorstop. Old console televisions become stands for newer sets, and novice do-it-yourselfers use chisels and screwdrivers to open paint cans. Thousands of computer veterans never master even a portion of the capabilities of their software programs, and many continue to treat the computer as an electronic typewriter.

Companies are often surprised to discover how their customers actually use their products and services. A poor understanding of the product results in underutilization or even misuse; thus, it is vital for the company to educate customers on proper usage.

Collaboration with core customers can help best-practice companies such as Black & Decker and Peapod develop new products, refine existing ones, and deal with service issues as they arise.

BLACK & DECKER COMPANY

When Black & Decker first came out with its VersaPak innovation (as described in chapter 4), customers were just starting to understand the concept of rechargeable batteries in tools for everyday use. Although the technology had existed for some time, the company was the first to offer an interchangeable battery that could be used for a number of tools. People were skeptical about whether such a product could deliver.

To educate those customers, Black & Decker sent out teams of engineers, marketers, and salespeople to show people how to use the new products. Parking their VersaPak van outside a Wal-Mart or other store, the teams invited customers to come onboard and try out cordless hedge trimmers and grass shears on real shrubs and pieces of sod. "They were a little bit hesitant that a cordless could do the job," says Mike Brennan, vice president for consumer products at Black & Decker. "We needed to show them." Once convinced that the product could deliver, customers bought a VersaPak for themselves.

Peapod, Inc.

To entice and keep busy consumers shopping for groceries over the Internet, Peapod, Inc. (first discussed in chapter 5), puts a heavy emphasis on its ability to establish a "learning relationship" with its customers. Peapod's belief that more and more of today's dual-income, stressed-out families will soon be choosing to shop online rather than wait in line appears warranted: Industry experts predict home shopping may represent as much as 20 percent of all grocery volume by 2003. That's a potential $80 billion market, and Peapod aims to be its leader by giving customers as much personal attention as possible.

The longer the company does business with each of its online clients, the more accurately its database discerns their shopping needs. The checkout clerk or deli manager at the local supermarket may recognize a customer's face, but Peapod knows when that person has bought Skippy peanut butter four times in a row—and would appreciate a coupon with his or her next order. Customer clients utilizing the company's Informix database can arrange their shopping lists by product category or pricing factors (such as what's on sale), or by such nutritional considerations as fat, calories, and cholesterol. When a product has been ordered three consecutive times, it automatically appears on a "shopping list" the next time the client signs on.

"Customers can identify what products they like or what nutritional factors are important to them, then put it on a personal list for future use," explains Peapod CEO and founder Andrew Parkinson. "The next time they come on the system, they can go right to the personal list and find or buy what they want. They end up being able to shop in ten or fifteen minutes."

Clients specify which substitution items they want to buy in case their product is out of stock, and Peapod's shopping crew takes care of the rest. Each order carries a 100 percent money-back guarantee, and complaints are recorded in the database and sorted by type to help the company analyze which areas need improvement. Coupons or other value-added materials are offered according to client buying patterns and personal preferences. "We target by individual household, not general demographics," says Parkinson. "It can be any attribute we like: what you've bought in the past, where you live, whether you typically redeem coupons, or anything else."

Much of this detailed knowledge about customers is gleaned electronically for use in Peapod's database. Its Universal Event Processor (UEP) technology enables Peapod to partner with marketing companies to advertise specific products online based on crucial information: whether a customer already purchases that product exclusively, buys a competitor's product, or shows no brand loyalty. Because the Peapod system is usually activated only when a client is ready to *place* an order, the marketing partner knows its ads, tie-in events, or sampling offers will reach consumers at their crucial moment of decision.

If a customer is about to select Pantene shampoo, for instance, an ad for Finesse shampoo promoting a 40-cent rebate may come up on the screen; additional content pages on Finesse can be linked to the ad, and all fulfillment and clearance details are handled by Peapod. As Parkinson sees it, everyone involved has his or her needs met. Peapod and its marketing partner both reach their customers one-on-one, and customers receive only those online promotions most likely to interest them.

"Kraft might come to us and say they want to target a new product to a certain type of consumer," says Parkinson. "We ask the criteria, and they say people who buy peanut butter and potato chips. We can deliver a sample of this new product to those households, see if they buy it, then hit them with a survey to find out what they did or didn't like about it. From all the knowledge we gain about consumers, we can provide them with the kind of products they like to buy and the information they want to read. We can even offer recipes to people who say they want them."

Subprocess 3 Measure Customer Performance and Satisfaction

Traditionally, a company has viewed its performance by conducting yearly or quarterly audits, measuring financial return on assets, or noting the rise in its stock price. There is obvious value in this kind of measurement, of course, but it means little to the average customer, who views the company's performance very differently. That individual is concerned less with the results of activity-based costing and financial results than with prompt order fulfillment and damage-free delivery. The customer is further impressed by how courteously and efficiently a service representative handles a complaint or whether an inquiry about a bill is processed without delay. In many industries, perhaps the majority, those criteria even outrank price, and where there is little to distinguish one company's products and services from the competition's, the customer will come down on the side of quality service—even if it means having to pay more for the item.

Best-practice companies constantly look for ways to measure customer performance and satisfaction. In putting this subprocess into action, those companies rely on both internal operating measures (for example, financial audits) and external methods such as collecting information about customers and tracking their perception of the company's quality and reliability.

By installing front-line measurement systems, a company can collect both customer data and feedback in real time. Sales representatives or customer service agents record whether a customer is displeased with a product simply by attaching the complaint to an update of the customer's file. For example, whenever an Orange County Teachers Federal Credit Union (FCU) representative interviews a member to gather updated information, he or she can pull up a new screen for recording any complaints and routing them immediately to the appropriate department or cross-functional team.

Following the example of best-practice companies, management should adopt a clear and comprehensive definition of "customer satisfaction." Although the definition will vary from company to company, nearly all will agree that the measure incorporates criteria such as the following:

- *Value-in-use* includes both functional and intangible attributes of the product or service. Customers want products that are reliable, easy to use, and suitable for the job. Glitz and chrome might capture a car buyer's attention for the moment, but such frills are unlikely to ring up lasting sales or make a customer loyal over the long term.

- *Critical incidents* include every point of direct contact between the company and the customer, and each one helps shape the customer's opinion of the relationship. These points of contact involve delivery, telephone calls requesting information, store visits, and repair calls. If the company representative is helpful, patient, courteous, and efficient, chances are great that the customer will respond in like fashion.

- *Customer-company relationships* can suffer when critical incidents fizzle or when customers perceive little or no value in using the company's products and services. Client companies often prefer a strong relationship with a few suppliers rather than weak relationships with many suppliers. And customers, whether they are individuals or large corporations, are no different in this respect: Both demand that the supplier share those values that they as customers hold, including reliability of performance, consistent pricing, personal recognition, respect, and the willingness to perform astounding feats of customer service.

As a best-practice organization, the Orange County Teachers FCU goes beyond the narrow definition of customer satisfaction as merely resolving complaints. When CEO Rudy Hanley says that Orange County Teachers FCU "delights the customer," he is not merely giving lip service to an overused term. Looking at both internal and external measures of customer satisfaction, the company always seeks to understand the key factors that customers value most.

ORANGE COUNTY TEACHERS FEDERAL CREDIT UNION

What happens when a customer who has a mediocre credit history decides to take a leave of absence from a teaching job to pursue a graduate degree and asks for a $22,000 loan that she cannot begin to repay for twelve months?

If the lending organization is a typical bank or mortgage company, the first and only response is likely to be a rejection of the applicant's request. If the lender is the Orange County Teachers FCU, the loan officer will look for another tactic. Indeed, as president and CEO Rudy Hanley says, "This case actually occurred. Our member had been turned down by other institutions, including banks. But we felt that while her credit risk was higher than we liked, the good social purpose of the loan and the fact that the member seeking it was someone our company was created to serve made approving it an acceptable risk we were willing to take." Whereas banks and mortgage companies are in the business to make a profit, Orange County Teachers FCU has a different set of priorities. Heading its agenda are outstanding service and members' complete satisfaction.

Ranking ninth in assets, as measured by Sheshunoff's 1997 survey of 11,572 credit unions in the United States, Orange County Teachers FCU serves 150,000 Orange County teachers, school administrators, staff employees, and their families. In its class, it is the fifth largest holder in the United States of home mortgages, and the company enjoys a response rate of 91 percent of its members, who report that the service is "good" or "excellent." (The next highest competitor has a rating of about 80 percent.)

Orange County Teachers FCU maintains its competitive advantage by thoroughly understanding the key factors driving customer satisfaction. Although, like other credit unions, the company is competitive on rates, it looks to other measures to distinguish itself and build loyalty among members. It creates this differentiation by tracking members and gathering data on their responses to its services.

In the credit industry, lenders measure customer performance through internal operating statistics such as increases in the number of new loans, the total volume of outstanding loans for new automobiles or homes, annual growth, return on assets, and member retention rates. Without benefit of a merger or the need to broaden its member base beyond the teaching profession, Orange County Teachers FCU has achieved an average growth in membership of 12 percent and an 18 percent increase in assets annually since 1985. Over the same period the company reports an average return on assets of 1.75 percent and has maintained a 13 percent capital ratio.

But as Hanley notes, these internal operating measures of success, based on financial ratios and growth, are insufficient by themselves to give a true picture of customer satisfaction. He believes that the customer-focused company should look beyond traditional financial measures to identify the factors that members care about most. This is not to say that financial statistics hold interest only for company auditors and stockholders, but competitive advantage comes to the company that looks in two directions: Financial audits tell managers and stakeholders where the company has been, whereas customer surveys tell them where the company should be heading. True, they should keep an eye on past performance, whether that of the previous quarter or the last decade, but they should also understand how their customers measure value and direct the company's forward progress accordingly.

Hanley and senior managers at Orange County Teachers FCU satisfy this second requirement by gathering information about customer satisfaction through random bimonthly surveys of two thousand members. Each questionnaire offers a member the chance not merely to tick off items on a wish list but also to respond discursively to issues of customer service and satisfaction.

In addition, since the early 1990s, Orange County Teachers FCU has outsourced some of its surveying to an outside company, Member Research, which provides a biannual survey of both Orange County Teachers FCU members and those of other credit unions. This comparative data gives Orange County Teachers FCU managers a clear picture of how the company stacks up against other credit unions emphasizing service. Since it began participating in the Member Research evaluation, Orange County Teachers FCU has been rated the top credit union in each member service area measured.

"We're obsessed with measuring member satisfaction and finding ways to improve it," says Hanley. "We conduct monthly phone surveys, biannual satisfaction surveys, and mystery shopper programs in which we pay members to complete extensive surveys based on their dealings with the company. All these programs work in tandem."

Unlike many other credit companies, Orange County Teachers FCU does not make it a point to delve deeply into its members' personal histories and financial status. It does gather basic statistics about a member's financial condition, but the company focuses more on the member's needs in order to establish a level of risk that it is willing to undertake. It then looks for ways to help that member satisfy its credit guidelines. As Hanley reports, the credit union adopts the attitude "Just Say Yes." Roughly translated, that slogan means that if it is in any way feasible for Orange County Teachers FCU to make a loan to a member, it will do so.

A recently divorced teacher, for example, applied for a renewal of her car lease but was turned down by the financial institution that originally issued the loan. The sole provider for her child, this teacher had a poor credit history and no clear means of repaying the loan on schedule. Orange County Teachers FCU realized, however, that the car was her only means of maintaining a livelihood and reestablishing good credit. "When you go above and beyond for customers," says Hanley, "they will repay you."

Indeed, this is exactly what happens at Orange County Teachers FCU. Whereas the average delinquency rate among its credit union peers is approximately 0.8 percent, Orange County Teachers FCU in mid-1997 registered a mere 0.41 percent. Its loan losses in the same period were 0.3 percent, half the industry average and approximately one-quarter that of banks. As Hanley points out, "Hundreds of members who are cleared of debts with Orange County Teachers FCU by declaring bankruptcy still pay us back."

Design and build customer profiles using a common database to track customer information. As American Express demonstrates, a complete and flexible database allows a company to capture significant information about customers and merchants, thereby controlling this three-way relationship by virtue of its involvement in each transaction.

Collect observations about customer preferences from point-of-contact employees who serve as "listening posts," as the Ritz-Carlton does.

Communicate customer information throughout the company. By using the chain's extensive database, each Ritz-Carlton hotel can combine its own employees' observations with those from employees who encountered the same guests on visits to other Ritz-Carlton hotels. This process helps the company prepare for guests' visits and secure long-term relationships.

Establish service information by studying how customers use (or misuse) products and services. Black & Decker discovered that it could actually instruct customers how best to use its VersaPak product, thereby altering customers' perceptions and ensuring sales. Peapod, Inc., on the other hand, finds that by understanding customers' buying patterns and preferences, it can capture present and future sales.

Gauge customer performance and satisfaction through both internal measures such as sales growth and revenues, and external ones such as industry analyses and customer surveys. As the Orange County Teachers FCU shows, it is possible to preserve customers' privacy while simultaneously establishing acceptable levels of risk and tracking how the company ranks against its competitors in terms of customer satisfaction.

1. Do you know your customers' purchasing patterns so well that you can pinpoint *when* they will likely make their next purchase of one of your products? Are you holding your breath, or are you taking a jar of Skippy off the shelf as Peapod is doing?

2. Do you study customer profiles to determine *how much* individuals are willing or likely to spend for products or services?

3. *Where* will customers make their next purchase of one of your products? At a discount store, through a catalog, over the Internet? Will you be there to make the sale wherever the order occurs?

4. Can you track customer preferences and how they change over time? If so, what do you do with this information?

5. What means do you have for collecting, organizing, and sharing customer data with people throughout your company? Why do you want to keep your people in the dark?

6. Are you constantly surprising and delighting customers with your products and services? How do you know?

7. How do *you* build long-term loyalty?

8. Does your organization have the capability for identifying customers to target with promotions specific to their needs? Can you find fans of a particular merchant or product as adeptly as American Express?

9. Can you deal with "ugly guests" as effectively as the Ritz-Carlton does?

10. Does your company try to educate customers in the proper use of products and services as Black & Decker does, or do you pray they'll educate themselves?

THE BALL'S IN YOUR COURT

Putting Best Practices to Work for You

Whether a company makes toasters or furnishes complicated telecommunications systems, its customers are likely to demand personalized, point-of-contact service. When they need help, they want to know their company contact specialists by first name, fax number, and personal telephone extension. As customers become more used to the kind of excellent service they receive from Dell Computer Corporation or The Walt Disney Company, they will not put up for long with an organization that cannot respond to their complaints quickly and efficiently.

As we first suggested in chapter 1, we believe that in its development of the Global Best Practices knowledge base, Arthur Andersen has uncovered a simple process-based framework that companies can use to meet the needs of both their current and future customers. The search for best practices can help those companies become more competitive in their business dealings with customers, particularly when they understand that, in essence, business is most simply defined as "people in relationships, performing processes." *People* means human beings with a strong desire to be successful, *relationships* means key stakeholder relationships (customer, employee, supplier, owner, society), and *processes* means the steps performed to achieve a desired result.

In today's world, sales and profits are essential if one wants to stay in business, but to be truly competitive in today's market, an organization looks to other key measures of success. We are convinced that one of the most important of these measures is customer satisfaction, and as we have stated throughout this book, that satisfaction—and its end result, loyalty—rest primarily on the degree to which customers are involved in the entire ownership experience (which, of course, begins even before someone makes an actual purchase). Black & Decker brings potential customers into the "classroom" of its promotion trucks to teach them how to use its VersaPak line of rechargeable tools. Varian Associates partners with its customers to solve problems with engineering new products. Holy Cross Hospital solicits comments from its customers and through its commando team seeks to overcome any obstacles to their comfort.

Customers form but one group of a company's stakeholders. In addition, employees, suppliers and distributors, owners, stockholders, and the society at large all have an abiding interest in what a company does and how it does it. A large part of what it means to do business is conveyed in the quality of the relationships that a company forms with each of these major stakeholders.

In today's competitive business environment, companies must decide, often at some cost, what kinds of relationships they want to have with customers and various other stakeholders. Some may—at their peril—prefer arm's-length, minimal associations. However, best-practice companies such as American Express, United Airlines, and Fingerhut go out of their way to identify their best customers and reward them for their loyalty. Others such as Allegiance Healthcare and GE Plastics partner with their customers to assist them in handling inventories, streamlining business functions, and improving efficiency and productivity.

Perhaps the key element that defines a good business relationship is *trust*. Best-practice companies seem to capitalize on the major benefit of strong relationships. A strong relationship results in trust, which further results in better communication—the lifeblood of world-class process performance.

When an acute care hospital invites Allegiance Healthcare personnel to occupy a section of its facility, monitor supplies, access information, and work directly with its own staff, that degree of intimacy points to a strong relationship based on trust. The hospital staff has confidence that Allegiance Healthcare takes its work as seriously as doctors and nurses take theirs and that when the need arises for special products, those items will be available to the people who need them. Trust needs more than reliability, however. It is grounded in the belief that two parties pursue compatible goals and hold like-minded values.

If strong relationships—like the best marriages—are based on trust, they are enhanced by clear, purposeful communication that is shared by all parties. In chapter 1, we defined the need for the "language" of process. To speak this language, a company should focus not on specific business functions such as developing products, manufacturing them, and processing orders, but on recognizing that each major customer service process discussed in this book results from a thoroughly orchestrated effort by everyone in a company to do what is necessary to satisfy a customer's needs from the beginning to the end of the buyer's experience. That effort requires communication.

A great conductor can signal a change in tempo with a flick of the baton, just as a great soloist can communicate with the orchestra by a sudden deep breath or a nod of the head. But however good the communication *within* the orchestra, there has to be an audience—a customer, if you will—to hear it and understand the music that is produced. For the best communication to take place, all parties—conductor, soloist, orchestra, and audience—need to understand the same language. And in great performances the distinction between what goes on "inside" the orchestra and who is "outside" of it seems to disappear. That, after all, is the effect of communication when it works at its best.

We need not press this analogy any further other than to point out that when a company and its customers speak the language of process, they too can overcome the barriers of "inside" and "outside." Just as the online grocer Peapod, Inc., knows not only what items its customers prefer but also *when* they are likely to purchase them, the best-practice company communicates so effectively with its customers that it can anticipate future needs and be ready with solutions whenever a problem arises. This is the essence of communication as illustrated by SARCOM's six-step process for clarifying customer expectations, reviewing the customer's problem on-site, solving it, and measuring the customer's satisfaction.

Our study of best-practice companies suggests that the superior way to reach the goal of complete customer focus and satisfaction is to study the actions currently being undertaken by companies of many different sizes that are flourishing in many different industries. By examining the history and refinement of each basic universal process, managers at any company in any industry can discover more innovative and effective ways of solving their current business problems and responding to their customers' needs.

Imaginatively transforming another company's success into one of your own requires a thorough understanding of all aspects of the market you are trying to reach, including both downstream and upstream participants. Indeed, all best-practice companies maximize their relationships with each of their stakeholders by constructing and executing such world-class processes.

While *Best Practices* focuses on customer processes—particularly how a best-practice company understands the needs of those customers, captures new ones, and develops loyalty—the customer relationship is only one in the vast network of a company's business processes and practices. How an organization attracts, wins, and serves its customers affects how it recruits, trains, and rewards its employees. How it manages information related not just to creating customer profiles but also to optimizing business functions on a global scale affects how that company satisfies stockholders and owners. How it manages its financial and physical resources has a lasting impact on how it positions itself for future growth. And how the company manages its relationship with the community at large has an important effect on how well it manages improvements and change within its own walls. As the companies featured in this book illustrate, an unwavering focus on customers—*understanding markets and customers; designing, marketing, selling, producing, and delivering products and services; as well as providing customer service*—can help put any business on the path to success.

A company that learns how to speak the language of process, builds relationships of trust with stakeholders, and is proactive rather than reactive with the forces of change will create value for both itself and its customers.

INDEX

CREDITS

This book makes references to various trademarks, marks, and registered marks owned by The Walt Disney Company and Disney Enterprises, Inc.

TOUCHSTONE

SIMON &
SCHUSTER

LEAN THINKING

Banish waste and create wealth in your corporation

James P. Womack and Daniel T. Jones

*'An inspiring, readable and thoroughly practical guide to
accelerating performance improvement in any industry'*
Sir John Egan, Chairman, BAA

After years of downsizing and re-engineering, most companies
are still searching for a formula for sustainable growth and
success. Using the principles of 'lean thinking' can breathe new
life into any company or economic activity, doubling
productivity and sales while stabilizing employment. Now this
groundbreaking book provides a step-by-step action plan based
on in-depth studies of 50 lean companies around the world,
including Unipart, Tesco, Toyota, Porsche and Pratt & Whitney.
For those who have already embraced lean thinking, it shows
how a further leap forward is possible. *Lean Thinking* offers a
new way of thinking, being and doing for every manager - one
that will change the world.

£8.99

0 684 81976-7

**SIMON &
SCHUSTER**

DELIVERING ON THE PROMISE

How to Attract, Manage and Retain Human Capital

Brian Friedman, James Hatch and David M. Walker

Over the past couple of decades, management styles have evolved from strategic planning to total quality management to re-engineering. Now, in the newest and most cost-effective trend to hit the boardrooms, there is a concentrated effort to view employees not as a perishable resource to be consumed but as a valuable commodity to be developed.

Delivering on the Promise reveals, for the first time, Arthur Andersen's proprietary, technically-based methodology - called the Five Squared Approach - that will enable any manager to measure, manage and leverage human capital Based on studies of such wide-ranging organisations as Shell Oil and British Airways, this book is an invaluable resource for CEOs, human resource directors and line managers.

'This book will help any company to help themselves'
Sir Peter Walters, Chairman SmithKline Beecham

PRICE £17.99
ISBN 0 684 8565 1

SIMON & SCHUSTER
A VIACOM COMPANY

A SELECTED LIST OF BUSINESS BOOKS
AVAILABLE FROM SIMON & SCHUSTER

THE PRICES SHOWN BELOW WERE CORRECT AT THE TIME OF GOING TO PRESS. HOWEVER SIMON & SCHUSTER RESERVE THE RIGHT TO SHOW NEW RETAIL PRICES ON COVERS WHICH MAY DIFFER FROM THOSE PREVIOUSLY ADVERTISED IN THE TEXT OR ELSEWHERE.

☐ 0 684 81976 7	Lean Thinking	*James P. Womack, Daniel T. Jones*	£8.99
☐ 0 684 85658 1	Delivering On The Promise	*Brian Friedman, James Hatch, David M. Walker*	£17.99
☐ 0 684 85839 8	The 7 Habits of Highly Effective People	*Stephen R. Covey*	£10.99
☐ 0 671 85323 6	The 7 Habits of Highly Effective People (audio)	*Stephen R. Covey*	£8.99
☐ 0 671 69765 X	Unlimited Power (audio)	*Anthony Robbins*	£8.99
☐ 0 671 85645 6	Excellence In The Organisation (audio)	*Tom Peters, Robert Townsend*	£9.99
☐ 0 671 85611 1	Maximum Achievement (audio)	*Brian Tracy*	£8.50
☐ 0 671 51226 9	The One Minute Manager (audio)	*Kenneth Blanchard PHD, Spencer Johnson*	£8.99
☐ 0 671 03339 5	Peak Performance In Practice (audio)	*Jim Steele*	£8.99

All Simon & Schuster titles are available by post from:

Book Service By Post, P.O. Box 29, Douglas, Isle of Man IM99 1BQ

Credit cards accepted. Please telephone 01624 675137, fax 01624 670923, Internet http://www.bookpost.co.uk or e-mail: bookshop@enterprise.net for details.

Free postage and packing in the UK. Overseas customers allow £1 per book (paperbacks) and £3 per book (hardbacks).